2-

Better Change

Best Practices for Transforming Your Organization

Better Change
Best Practices for Transforming Your Organization

THE PRICE WATERHOUSE CHANGE INTEGRATION® TEAM

Irwin Professional Publishing
Burr Ridge, Illinois
New York, New York

Photo credits: p. 37, Copyright of Image Bank/(Steve Neidorf); p. 40, Copyright of Image Bank/(Williamson/Edwards); p. 56, Copyright of Image Bank/(Tim Bieber Inc.); p. 72, Copyright of Image Bank/(TTTC Productions); p. 108, Copyright of Image Bank/(Mark Romanelli); p. 120, Copyright of Image Bank/(Stephen Derr); p. 136, Copyright of Image Bank/(Jay Freis); p. 160, Copyright of Image Bank/(David W. Hamilton); p. 178, Copyright of Image Bank/(Steve Neidorf)

Senior sponsoring editor: Amy Hollands Gaber
Project editor: Jane Lightell
Production manager: Bob Lange
Designer: Heidi J. Baughman
Art coordinator: Mark Malloy
Compositor: Electronic Publishing Services, Inc.
Typeface: 12/14 Times Roman
Printer: Von Hoffmann Press

Library of Congress Cataloging–in–Publication Data

Better change : best practices for transforming your organization /
   The Price Waterhouse Change Integration Team.
      p.   cm.
   Includes index.
   ISBN 0-7863-0342-5
      1. Organizational change.   2. Organizational effectiveness.
   I. Price Waterhouse (Firm).   Change Integration Group.
   HD58.8.B49   1995
      658.4'063—dc20

                                            94–10542

Printed in the United States of America
   3 4 5 6 7 8 9 0 VH 1 0 9 8 7 6 5 4

Foreword

Most of us in business are probably of two minds about books on business. On the one hand, each of us surely can remember a few books that made a difference—showed us how to do something important we had never done before or how to think along fresh lines about something that matters. On the other hand, business is a pragmatic exercise—you learn it by doing it. Admittedly, there are many intellectual challenges; products and services today tend to have high intellectual content. But most of us have more respect for astute action than for words, more interest in sensible risk taking than in probability theory. We have done our very best to write a book that deserves to be read, and read carefully, by business executives who have time for substance but none for fluff. The topic is probably the central concern of our business era: change. We suspect your organization is being buffeted by winds of change. We are certain that the great organizations of the years ahead will be those that master the process of change. Many executives understand this and are working hard to build competency in the management of change. That is what our book is for: building the skills of those who seek to drive change into and through their organizations.

The dynamics that spawn change initiatives in large organizations involve three major factors. Senior executives press strategic intent from the top. When they do so effectively, they drive a common vision and shared commitment throughout the organization. The second factor is high-initiative, entrepreneurial managers—people who continuously look for ways to make significant improvements in their operations. They push change ideas up to senior management and down to the functional groups for which they are responsible. The third factor is the many managers and employees operating within the strategic context established by senior executives, laboring day by day to get the work done. This all-important population (managers and the work force) tends to filter and dilute both the strategic call to arms from the executive suite and many of the innovations championed by entrepreneurial managers. The degree of influence each of these parties brings to change is a function of many things, including the leadership skills of the CEO, his or her ability to communicate a vision that resonates with employees, and the value placed by the culture on innovation and initiative.

Out of the struggle among these sometimes competing forces are born the many performance improvement initiatives under way in organizations today. These programs or projects take many forms: reengineering, TQM, downsizing, activity-based costing, implementation of new technologies, and others. They all have much in common. They share the fundamental objective of improving the performance of the organization, however defined and measured. They also share a moderately revolutionary flavor: to achieve the targeted improvements, the organization must undergo some degree of transformation involving processes, organizational structures, technologies, and so on.

Making those transformations happen is what this book is about. It is a guide for everyone initiating, leading, participating in, or impacted by change initiatives. Its ideas and pragmatic how-to suggestions are supported by nearly 100 anecdotes and case studies. The book is a tool kit.

THE SCIENCE OF CHANGE—AND ITS APPLICATION

The science of managing change and implementing serious improvements in large organizations is evolving rapidly. Impelled by the enormous pressures on companies in the early 90s, there has been much good thinking about change. At this point, the first wave of change projects undertaken in a new spirit and under pressure is now past. We can all learn from the results of that first wave, and to convey what we believe has been learned is part of the mission of this book. We hope to make two further contributions to the growing body of knowledge on organizational change. First, by codifying and elaborating on the 15 guiding principles of *Better Change*, we wish to provide managers around the world with a convenient and effective guide for their performance improvement initiatives. We know of very few successful change programs that defied these principles.

The second contribution we seek to make is to give those sponsoring change a new attitude. Everyone has heard the expression: "He (or she) has an attitude." Our contention is that, to sponsor successful change, you do need an attitude, one that we don't see often enough. We describe this attitude in terms of four values:

A NEW LEVEL OF HONESTY

The emperor's clothes are strewn over the landscape of today's organizations. Too few business managers face reality and communicate candidly. Unfortunately, the pain and hard work accompanying real change necessitate a level of candor too many executives fail to achieve. Further, in deference to hurt feelings or employee morale, some managers deny reality, avoid confrontation, and communicate with spin control in high gear. Honesty and openness are fundamental in high-performance organizations. Use this book to build a new level of honesty into your organization's change initiatives.

A NEW LEVEL OF COURAGE

There is much talk of slaying sacred cows. Few are slain; most die of old age. The mandate for change is seldom bold enough to overcome entrenched obstacles to change. Life is full of choices. In large-scale organizational change, many tough decisions are encountered. Boldness is called for.

A NEW RESPECT FOR DIVERSITY

The work force is changing. Brilliant managers who happen to be women, minorities, or foreign nationals are becoming major players in US companies today, and their numbers are increasing. However, too few change leaders at present draw from the diversity of ideas and perspectives represented by these individuals to enrich the process of change. Change is all about creativity. Use every tool you can to create a firestorm of new thinking.

A NEW SENSITIVITY TO ALL STAKEHOLDERS

Just as markets are being continually refined into narrower and more specific segments, your change program will need to segment stakeholders and stakeholder groups and acknowledge their concerns.

You may be wondering where we learned our lessons—among them, the lesson that there is always more to learn! The case studies in this book are based on Price Waterhouse engagements with major corporations worldwide. We have learned from those experiences. And then we have had to apply the principles of organizational transformation to our own firm, which is no more sheltered from stiff competitive pressures than any other business today. Price Waterhouse is changing because, like you, we must change.

We want you to *use* this book, even use it up. Write on the pages—the margins are wide for that reason. Use the bookmarks we've provided in the back. The system of graphic icons will refer you to other chapters where more information is available on a given topic. There is even a postcard so that we can hear your news from the front. This book is our news. Let us hear from you!

Bill Dauphinais (New York)
Paul Pederson (Dallas)
The Price Waterhouse Change Integration® Team

THE AUTHORS

G. William Dauphinais

Paul O. Pederson

Henry G. Adamany, Jr.

Kevin M. Bacon

George Bailey

Thomas W. Britton, Jr.

Thomas P. Colberg

Edmund O. Goll

James M. Holec, Jr.

Daniel P. Keegan

Mark D. Lutchen

Richard A. Moran, Ph.D.

William M. Noonan

James M. Prendergast

Colin N. Price

William T. Reeves

Acknowledgments

An undertaking of the scope of this book is not a solo journey. In addition to the collaborating group of authors listed on the previous page, we have benefited from the skill and perseverance of a number of outstanding editorial and design professionals.

At Irwin Professional Publishing, we have benefited from the knowledge and talents of more people than we could possibly mention. Michael Desposito saw the merits of our project before we had much of merit to show him. Jeffrey Krames has been a friend to our effort from the beginning. Our editor, Amy Hollands Gaber, joined the team as the manuscript was being polished and has ably served as our principal contact with Irwin Professional Publishing. The Irwin design team, headed by Heidi Baughman, demonstrated both plenty of talent and plenty of patience as the team helped us realize our dream of a communication that is a good deal more than just words on the page.

Contributions were made by many at Price Waterhouse. The following people contributed their wisdom through cases and counsel:

Michael Cordovano	Mike Corley
Randy Dalia	Bill Ek
Andy Embury	Richard Gane
Tig Gilliam	William Gillmour
Daniel Hirschbueler	Kurt Janvrin
Charles Kalmbach	Charles Keeling
Robert Leach	Alan Little
Joe Marino	Frank Marsteller
Randy McAdams	David Miller

Quentin Morelle   Eamonn Murphy

David Narrow   Clive Newton

Tim Ogilvie   Jack Pastor

Glen Peters   Denis Picard

Cedric Read   Jeff Redfield

Bob Russell   John Sharlacken

John Simke   Scott Smith

Nicole Willenz Gardner

Tammerie Spires of our Dallas office has been both a contributor of ideas and a skilled manager of thousands of details, any one of which if neglected could mar the finished communication. Rosemary Martinez, who designs publications for our Dallas office, has left her stylish mark on the book layout.

The firm's director of external communications, Roger Lipsey, contributed mightily as a writer and editor to the project as a whole.

Table of Contents

CHAPTER ONE

The Basics of Change

The earliest surviving book, by some accounts, is the ancient Chinese **Book of Changes**. That book remains interesting. It proposes a matrix of 64 distinct circumstances, dissects them with stunning lucidity, and recommends actions to capture the greatest benefit or minimize difficulty. It is in some ways a book of magic, but even more so a first, grand attempt by the human race to develop a science of change. The virtues it endorses—attentiveness, flexibility, perseverance, awareness of where others stand in a given circumstance—will serve well today. Corporate executives across US industry are confronting the needs of their organizations and considering how to improve organizational performance. A science of change, even a little magic, would be helpful: Large-scale change is never easy to achieve, and there are many traps. Our book will put before you as much science as possible, many tips, and we hope a little magic. The best magic of all is confidence—confidence that you understand how others have succeeded (and where they failed), confidence in a proven method to initiate change processes and see them through to success. In the **Book of Changes**, the 64 distinct circumstances tend to flow freely into one another. If you get out your calculator and compute the possible permutations when one circumstance can flow into just one other at a given time, you will see what the ancients felt they were up against. Conditions are no simpler in today's hard-pressed businesses.

• • •

Our title, *Better Change*, cuts two ways. On the one hand, it is an admonition. In light of the condition of many American businesses, there is no reason to apologize for sounding the alarm: Better change—and change now! On the other hand, it is a promise that we mean to keep. Our author group hopes to provide readers of this book with a better, experience-corrected approach to envisioning, initiating, supporting, defending, and successfully completing ambitious change programs in your organization.

On the admonitory side, there is clearly cause for worry among US business leaders, and for remedial action. Failure to rework our businesses in acutely intelligent and forceful ways can lead to—or tolerate the persistence of—lagging performance, low employee morale, and shareholder disillusion. We have all been astonished by the humbling of industrial giants whose competitive positions seemed unassailable. Such companies first ceded ground slowly to nimble upstarts, then were pushed to the brink, and now struggle to reinvent themselves. Their publicized ordeals are only the most visible sign of a period of fundamental challenge through which many, many businesses are passing.

To our minds, the key entrepreneurial exercise of our time is to envision and implement large-scale change that generates dramatically better levels of performance. An important part of this exercise is to discover these opportunities for performance-building change not only where you would expect to find them (such as product/service innovation and cost control) but also in the hidden recesses of the business where so much is quietly at stake (such as interdepartmental communication and patterns of authorization). The Big Idea, as we argue in Chapter Eight, is often a network of small but powerful ideas that have been lingering, untried, for some time. It is a terrific thing to invent and market the Walkman.

FIGURE 1.1
THE OPPORTUNITY

Successful companies continually respond to changing customer needs and the changing competitive environment. However, outmoded business practices, organizational boundaries, cultural impediments, functional versus customer view of problems, and a legacy of aging systems technology often constrain much of the change companies actually implement. Over time, these constraints lead to what can be a significant gap between potential and actual performance. You cannot afford this performance gap.

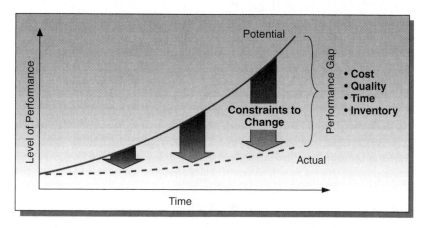

CHAPTER ONE

It is also a terrific thing to build an organization with cat-quick responsiveness to customer needs and the means and skills to work together to satisfy those needs better than any other organization in the world.

Change occasions possibility. Your instincts, like ours, probably tell you that out of the turbulence in today's business landscape will emerge new champions of wholly redefined industries. High-performance organizations are changing rapidly—redefining their boundaries, reengineering their processes, outsourcing nonstrategic activities, partnering with customers and suppliers as never before. The predictable playing field, in which companies could set a strategy and securely focus on its execution, is a thing of the past.

The admonition, Better change!, is meant to resonate throughout this book. But we will not spend much time trying to persuade you that significant change is imperative. Our expectation is that you already believe, perhaps passionately, that your organization must change, and change now. But while we believe that *you* are convinced, we do not assume that anyone around you fully shares your view. Very seldom is there consensus surrounding the need to change, much less concerning the magnitude of change required to meet—not merely to take a stab at meeting—your organization's objectives. Chapters Two and Three (respectively, "Building the Case for Change" and "Motivating Stakeholders") provide guidance on how to generate consensus among those within your organization who can be most instrumental in supporting or stalling the changes you seek. Those chapters should give you more than enough ammunition to take aim—for the ultimate benefit of all—at those you must compel to act.

> **Our expectation is that you already believe, perhaps passionately, that your organization must change, and change now. But while we believe that *you* are convinced, we do not assume that anyone around you fully shares your view.**

Most of the material in this book supports the second meaning of better change. It is a book about envisioning and managing change processes to transform today's organization. In this positive sense, we mean these things:

BETTER CHANGE . . .

- Is integral to and focused on your organization's strategy.
- Leads to high performance, dramatically improved results, and measurable differences.
- Is fueled by the brightest energy and most creative ideas of your people.

- Is supported by properly empowered and motivated employees.
- Is driven by specific customer needs.
- Is guided by a limited set of balanced performance measures.
- Builds revenue (i.e., it is not solely obsessed with cost).
- Is institutionalized in a culture that values continuous improvement.

15 Guiding Principles

The circumstances surrounding your change projects are unique to your situation. What you must do to transform *your* organization cannot be detailed precisely by any book. This is one of the challenges of change: There is no explicit calculus, no prescriptive outline of the steps you must hazard to drive change in your organization. However, our experience, drawn from hundreds of client assignments, points to a finite set of principles to which one *can* securely look to achieve better change. Our goal is to ably communicate these principles to you and to do so in a fashion that gives you the confidence and the will to act. We shall also illustrate through brief case studies how these principles have been applied—or ignored—in companies across the full range of industries. As you begin this journey or regroup for a better attempt at driving change in your organization, try to keep these principles in mind. The words we use to express them are not the important thing; put them in your own words. But the underlying ideas *are* important.

   1. Confront reality. All of us who have invested our lives in building successful organizations need to face a harsh reality: These structures—the products and services they offer, the processes and technologies that support them—are not reality by tomorrow's standards. We are all highly vested in the seductive notion that what we have built will continue to flourish. However, the new reality creeps up as new business models emerge and our competitiveness falters. Know this.

   2. Focus on strategic contexts. Most organizations are experiencing explosive change. Driven by global competition and incredibly fruitful technology innovations, this trend can only accelerate, and opportunities for change will be endless. However, capital and energy are not. Knowing *where* to invest in change—*where* to seek improved performance—will separate the victors from the vanquished. Focus your efforts where the payback will be greatest.

   3. Summon a strong mandate. Change must be supported by a strong mandate. This mandate is generally provided by top management, but it should be amplified by the voice of the customer. Without a strong and consistent mandate, you may double the cost of change and halve the impact.

4. Set scope intelligently. Setting an appropriate scope for your change effort is critically important. Focus on measurably improving performance in areas most important to the organization and its key stakeholders (e.g., owners, customers, and employees). If you overreach your change sponsor's broadest possible sphere of influence, you can fail. If you define a scope that is too limited, success may not matter.

5. Build a powerful case for change. You cannot assume others are prepared for change. It is seldom so. You will need to build a powerful case for change, then work relentlessly to generate consensus, beginning with executive management and radiating down and across the entire organization.

6. Let the customer drive change. The customer is your ally in building the case for change. Serving customers is a powerful common denominator in your organization; customers are the raison d'être of the organization. Their needs, rigorously examined, should dictate change.

7. Know your stakeholders. Powerful individuals and groups have stakes in the changes you're contemplating. You will need to segment, understand, and prioritize the needs and motives of these stakeholders.

> **If you overreach your change sponsor's broadest possible sphere of influence, you can fail. If you define a scope that is too limited, success may not matter.**

8. Communicate continuously. If your change program is to succeed, you must communicate continuously with stakeholders as changes are envisioned and implemented. Your case for change and style of communication must resonate with them, convince them to act anew. Clear, succinct messages will be understood. Honest messages will be believed.

9. Reshape your measures. Driving change, causing people to act anew will require you to examine carefully your organization's performance measures. Build your vision, then design new measures consistent with its strategies and goals. Take the time to reevaluate and, if necessary, dismantle old measures.

10. Use all of the levers of change. There are key points of application in your organization that will repay your efforts. These are the levers of change. Use them all: the markets and customers you pursue; product and service offerings; the organizational structure; human resources systems, including reward programs; business processes; and supporting technologies. Large-scale change can be achieved only when all of these levers are brought to bear in a coordinated manner.

11. Think big. The change leader must work tirelessly to persuade the change leadership team to think big and to draw positive innovations from people throughout the organization. Small thinking dominates many projects, with predictable results. People need to feel free to take the lid off, to think out of the box, to surface dozens of ideas that may not work in order to come up with a few that are genuinely powerful.

12. Leverage diversity. It is famously difficult to think out of the box, in part because we are the ones who built the box, and at the time it was an excellent box. An unparalleled opportunity for innovative thinking now awaits us as increasing numbers of women, minorities, and foreign nationals enter our organizations. These minds and perspectives help to shake the old paradigms and where necessary replace them.

13. Build skills. Overinvest in human capital. Build skills in your people at all levels. Broaden the technical, problem-solving, decision-making and leadership skills of those "in the trenches." Strengthen the facilitation, managerial, delegation, listening, communication, and diversity skills of those at the top. Make skill building a key performance measure for all employees.

14. Plan. To drive change, you must develop a documented and detailed action plan for change. It must cover all major actions required, including changes in processes, systems, people, organizational culture, the physical plant, the organizational structure, and training needs.

15. Integrate your initiatives. Change programs of one type or another bubble up continuously in high-performance organizations.

FIGURE 1.2
THE LEVERS OF CHANGE

Markets and customers

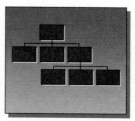
Structure and facilities

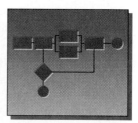
Business processes

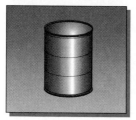
Products and services

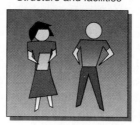
People
(and reward systems)

Technologies

Savvy executives strive to balance the entrepreneurship of high-initiative managers with the need to adhere to a focused strategy. As change programs emerge, define their objectives, and consume resources, it is critical to maintain a consistent, integrated rationale for the whole pattern of change. An unplanned patchwork of change initiatives will promote bitter competition for resources, confuse employees, and reduce the positive impact of any one initiative.

In the material ahead and in the following chapters, we will elaborate on these principles and show you how to work with them. Capitalize on what others have learned.

CHANGE WHAT?

Consider how your organization operates today. Now envision what it might be, could be, if your hopes are fulfilled. Imagine how it might operate far more successfully in the future. There is almost certainly a gap between the present and the future along a number of important dimensions. We have found it useful to formalize these dimensions through the concept, introduced a moment ago, of six "levers of change." As illustrated in Figure 1.2, the levers of change are:

> **Your vision may include differences in the kinds of people you will need, systems and measures for rewarding them, and the culture that sends them daily signals concerning "how we do business" and "what we are all about" as a company.**

• **Markets and customers.** Your vision of present and future may include differences in the way your organization will—or should—view and segment its markets and customer base.

• **Products and services.** The refined market focus you envision may be accompanied by changes in the scope and variety of products and services your organization seeks to bring to market. Perhaps you sense a need to establish strategic alliances and partnerships with key customers and suppliers.

• **Business processes.** There will probably be a gap in the way your company's business processes operate now and the way they will need to operate in the future to bring competitive products and services to market. You may already perceive the need to introduce a new set of pointedly relevant performance measures at the corporate and business unit levels.

• **People and reward systems.** Your vision may include differences in the kinds of people you will need, systems and measures for rewarding them, and the culture that sends them daily signals concerning "how we do business" and "what we are all about" as a company.

• **Structure and facilities.** There is probably a gap between the organization's structure today and its best future configuration. New facilities may also show up in your vision of the kind of future worth having.

• **Technologies.** Finally, your vision may reveal a gap between the information-based technologies in place today and those needed to remain competitive in the future.

The changes necessary to move the organization toward your vision of its strongest future are likely to involve change in all the above areas. This is so for the healthiest of companies; the need to change is not necessarily a sign of poor corporate health. Stasis, on the other hand, is invariably a bad sign.

SET YOUR SCOPE FOR HIGH-IMPACT SOLUTIONS

We often observe a discrepancy between the results expected of specially appointed change project teams and the authority and freedom of action conferred on the teams by senior managements. Senior executives typically want and work hard to promote "big" results. But they will get only what they make possible. Hence, two important questions that change teams and their senior executive sponsors need to clarify early: What is the scope of the project? How many levers of change may the team actually access and alter?

For example, can the change team recommend and secure approval for significant changes in the organizational structure—or is that option off-limits? Can the team make substantial changes in the degree to which frontline employees are empowered—or do union and human resource policy factors put this option out of bounds? Can the team suggest segmenting and serving customers in a completely new construct? Can it consider discontinuing less attractive or conflicting product lines? Is it free to consider new performance measures and reward systems?

The answers to these questions, each of which tests the limit in relation to the six levers of change, will generate a realistic sense of the agreed scope of a change effort. This in turn will enable or constrain the impact you can expect to achieve.

The top executives of a large manufacturing company recently attended a sophisticated seminar on business reengineering. All of them left the meeting excited about the breakthroughs possible through reengineering. Translating their excitement into action, they commissioned a team to lead a reengineering project with the objective of major performance improvement. However, the team was told: "Hands off organizational and incentive compensation issues." Performance measures were also just about off-limits. By the time the ground rules were laid, the team was authorized to reengineer in only two of the six real levers of change.

The project was a modest success. But management had not left the seminar dreaming of modest success. The team finished its work with the certainty that much more could have been achieved.

If you want the best results from your change effort, it must have the right scope. This may sound obvious, but setting scope and securing freedom of action appropriate to that scope are not simple matters. Is it a process, a department, or the whole company that needs to be retooled? If a process, have you examined it well enough to understand it? What boundaries does the process cross? Who are the major stakeholders? Is the team genuinely empowered to think big and to lay hands on all the levers of change?

One-dimensional change typically generates either modest improvement in the bottom line or outright failure that will tend to sour employees on change programs. Better change is always multidimensional. If you ask people for better performance, you must improve their work processes, give them access to the right information and tools, give them the authority to make decisions, measure performance in new ways, and reward them for higher performance.

> **If you redesign processes, you must also redesign jobs and procedures, change the systems and technologies that support these processes, train people to perform new or different tasks, and remove barriers to change.**

If you restructure the organization, you must also rethink processes and the line of command, ensure that the systems and technology infrastructure supports the new configuration, and revise performance evaluation and compensation to motivate adherence to the new structure.

If you redesign processes, you must also redesign jobs and procedures, change the systems and technologies that support these processes, train people to perform new or different tasks, and remove barriers to change.

If you invest in technologies such as information systems, you must also consider whether they support customer-critical processes and integrate with technologies now in place that you do not intend to upgrade. Further, you must prepare people to use the new technologies in their new or different jobs.

High-performance organizations address change in all of its dimensions. They involve parties not only throughout the organization but also beyond its boundaries. This multidimensional,

FIGURE 1.3
IS YOUR MANDATE
CLEAR?

Too often the mandate for change is not clear. It is not enough to talk in terms of broad objectives. These must be translated into real performance measures and corresponding stretch targets.

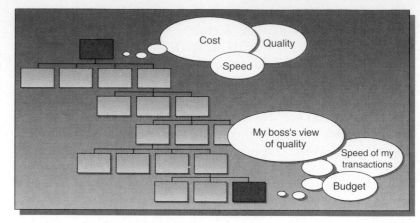

comprehensive approach offers the potential for dramatic performance improvement through solutions integrated across the company's entire product/service supply chain.

As we are writing, the more successful product companies are working with their suppliers, distributors, and customers to reengineer the multiple chains of activity coordinated by the companies. Forward-looking management teams recognize that the arena of change lies both within the company and outside in their key relationships with suppliers and distributors. An *integrated* solution will lower costs across the entire system of material supply, manufacture, and eventual distribution to the customer. This is working all the levers of change to good purpose.

CREATING A POWERFUL MANDATE FOR CHANGE

Every successful change project has a sponsor whose position becomes entwined with the success of the effort. The change team leader builds the case, sells it, marshals the necessary resources, sets goals, establishes milestones. The change team leader willingly becomes identified with the program in people's minds—when you pass this person in the hall, you know who he or she is and what he or she's doing. The team leader tirelessly reiterates the message of change throughout relevant parts of the organization to keep people focused on the big picture while they work the details. This visionary, almost evangelical, behavior—coupled with dogged determination to knock down every barrier—is the stuff of change leadership. If the right person for this challenge is not leading the effort, find the right one quickly or the effort is doomed.

Ask yourself these basic questions to evaluate the leadership of your change effort. Who is driving change into and through the organization? Is this person fully committed, even impassioned about the possibilities and about making them real? Is he or she genuinely in a position to influence others—or is more senior executive support needed? The potential for success lies within your answers to these questions.

A POWERFUL CASE FOR CHANGE IS IMPERATIVE

Unless and until your key audiences clearly understand *what* must change to achieve your vision, there is no reliable mandate. Recognition of the need for change often begins at senior management level. On the other hand, the wake-up call can come from customers or from departments that begin to feel intolerably hampered by a flawed process or productivity problems. Wherever the desire for change begins, it needs to spread throughout the organization, thanks to a powerfully communicated case for change.

Recently, the management of a large international oil company undertook a major process reengineering effort. Management believed that its rationale for the effort—and the associated organizational pain—was shared by most stakeholders. Management believed, to be specific, that everyone agreed on the importance of arresting and reversing the company's decline in rank as a revenue producer among the largest global oil companies. Unfortunately, many key stakeholders did not perceive a persuasive linkage between this measure of business performance and the need to go through personal upheaval and change. Few were convinced that overall ranking meant all that much—in fact, they questioned the validity of the statistic and could not see how improving business processes would directly impact the company's overall performance. This is a classic example of a partial mandate, tantamount to no mandate since, as events unfolded, the project foundered. Cherishing its own assumptions and perspective and failing to campaign among key stakeholders with unexpectedly different views, management had neglected to build the case for change.

> **This visionary, almost evangelical, behavior—coupled with dogged determination to knock down every barrier—is the stuff of change leadership.**

Things went otherwise at a global chemical manufacturer. The company had almost a century of tradition behind its customer service processes and organizational structure. This proud tradition was, from another perspective, so much mortar holding steep barriers to change in place. Although there was a degree of management interest in change, no significant change program could be mustered until outside market research interviews of all key customers revealed facts so compelling that they toppled resistance to reorganizing the business, process by process. The customer's view of the company provided the raw material for a strong case for change. The principal change leader shaped this raw material into a powerful case for change and communicated it widely and forcefully. He succeeded in gaining acceptance of his vision among all key stakeholders.

SOUND PERFORMANCE MEASURES DRIVE CHANGE

Conventional wisdom holds that change is basically a good thing, and that it is a continuous, unending process. This is probably true as far as it takes us—but all meaningful change projects have a beginning, middle, and end. Without a goal or target and quantitatively measurable milestones along the way, change efforts to improve business performance may quickly become slogans without substance. Setting a challenging target for the organization is key to sustaining support for the change, and score keeping is just as key.

Who are the key stakeholders in your change project? There are many, they differ from one another, and you need their support.

Examples of clearly defined, measurable targets abound. In the case of a large manufacturer of office supplies, the targets for a process reengineering effort were to fill all orders within 24 hours, achieving a line-item fill rate on each order of 95 percent. Progress toward this goal was tracked on a weekly basis and continues to this day. This mandate for change and its highly specific target could have been conceived and pushed by senior management. But it was not—it came directly from the organization's largest customer. The customer simply demanded this level of performance, and every stakeholder in the reengineering effort knew it. No one had a problem understanding the significance of achieving the targets: The future depended on it.

A large chemical company determined through market research that on-time delivery was the single most important factor driving customer satisfaction and repeat business. Penalties experienced by the customer for shipments delivered a day early or late were: no available railroad siding if early; plant closes if late. It was clear that on-time delivery should be the new measure driving performance and the new performance target could be nothing short of 100 percent on-time delivery. The company's people recognized they would have to do whatever was required to meet the goal: change processes, retrain and reeducate, redraft the organizational structure, replace technology—all to achieve the new performance level and retain customers.

BUILDING THE CONSENSUS FOR CHANGE AT THE TOP

It is essential to build consensus around the need for change at all levels of the organization—and to return frequently to your many audiences to check the health of that consensus and repair it where and when necessary. One key element in that consensus is a common understanding between top management and the project team: They must agree on the scope and desired outcomes of all project tasks. Further, so much is learned from implementing each project task that new insights are almost certain to suggest small or large course corrections as time goes on. This calls for frequent revisiting and consensus checking between top management and the change leaders who actually steer events. Common understanding and agreement at their level on the plan as a whole is essential not just at the beginning but also at all key milestones.

BUILDING THE CONSENSUS FOR CHANGE WITH STAKEHOLDERS

Who are the key stakeholders in your change project? There are many, they differ from one another, and you need their support. Without their support, you can dream of significant change but almost certainly can't achieve it. In Chapter Three ("Motivating Stakeholders"), you will find guidelines for identifying and segmenting your stakeholders to uncover selectively how they view the changes you're contemplating and what key wants and needs must be satisfied to secure their commitment to change.

Open and frank communications through both formal and informal channels facilitate consensus building. Feedback is critical for effective change management and to motivate people to support the coming changes. What is needed here are better listening skills, not necessarily better directive or control skills. Therefore, don't select your team solely on the basis of past project successes. Broad-based change will stretch even the best past performers.

Find good listeners and communicators—people who are willing to go out to the stakeholders, understand their perspectives, and encourage their participation in a persuasive but wholly honest way.

American author and publisher Elbert Hubbard once said: "The ideas that benefit a man are seldom welcomed by him on first presentation." Repeated, but not dull, communication is the *primary* means of gaining and increasing the commitment of stakeholders to the changes ahead. Successful organizations develop and carry out practical plans for communicating with stakeholders about the goals of change and the unfolding change process. They ensure that everyone in the organization is continuously informed and that involvement in the effort becomes a badge of honor.

In addition to conventional means of communicating (e.g., meetings, presentations, bulletin boards, newsletters), there are quite a few valid unconventional tactics for building consensus and solving consensus problems along the way. Going the extra mile to involve stakeholders in problem solving, knowledge sharing, and examining the progress and problems of the change effort always yields a better result. One large gas company took the change team members and key stakeholders through an abbreviated Outward Bound "ropes course" in which the participants learned to rely on each other in unfamiliar conditions. Another organization set up a hot line for all stakeholders—24 hours a day—to express concerns, surface information, and feed the communication process. Another established within its e-mail system an electronic bulletin board for stakeholder concerns.

Activities of this kind are necessary to influence mind set and motivation. For years, experienced project managers have intuitively used these types of communications vehicles. We recommend that your change project explicitly include these activities in the work plan and staff them appropriately to ensure the change process moves forward. (See Chapter Four, "Communicating Honestly," for a full discussion of communicating with stakeholders.)

THE IMPACT OF DIVERSITY

A core team is typically formed and given responsibility for managing and facilitating a change effort from start to finish. Clearly key to your project's success is the quality of this team. Implementing comprehensive change requires a mix of technical competencies, "home turfs," and personal styles. The team's makeup will depend on the business issues to be resolved and the scope of change envisioned, but it will certainly involve diverse disciplines, functions, and personal capacities, including:

Technology	Process redesign
Human resource development	Training development
Communications	Organizational restructuring
Interviewing and information gathering	Project planning
Change facilitation and implementation	Operation of business processes
Leadership	Negotiation and conflict resolution

Regardless of how carefully you select your team, you must still be prepared to alter its membership and size during the project. Depending on the need for specific skills, workload, or availability, team members may enter and exit. Further, it is common to spin off subteams responsible for implementing components of the vision. Also, you will probably find yourself facing some disappointments: Not every original member of the team will prove to have "the right stuff." Some may be not just provocative in their thinking but also obstructive; others may have signed on without fully recognizing the burden they were shouldering.

The majority of the team should be respected individuals from your organization. Consultants can help, but they should not dominate the team. When the team consists wholly of outsiders, stakeholders tend to perceive the change as imposed rather than welling up from internal recognitions of organizational needs—and they are not likely to buy in. Our research indicates that most successful change efforts draw the majority of their assigned talent from within the organization. These people should all be "movers and shakers" viewed by other employees as role models and as trustworthy, thoughtful leaders. The team members will be diverse in skill and personal style, but they should have this much in common: They have earned respect legitimately in your organization over time—and by "legitimately" we mean that, however forceful and energetic they may be, they are also sensitive to other people's needs and ideas.

> **Going the extra mile to involve stakeholders in problem solving, knowledge sharing, and examining the progress and problems of the change effort always yields a better result.**

FIGURE 1.4
DRIVING IDEAS INTO
DETAILED,
IMPLEMENTABLE ACTION
PLANS

Once the changes you seek have been designed, that design should be refined and driven down to a detailed level for implementation planning purposes. The plan will address the timing and responsibility for implementation and will set clear performance goals and timetables.

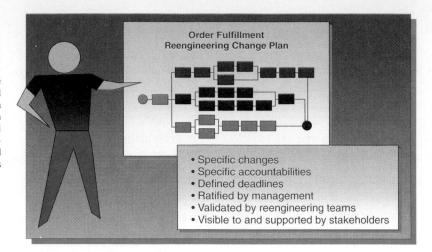

Order Fulfillment
Reengineering Change Plan

• Specific changes
• Specific accountabilities
• Defined deadlines
• Ratified by management
• Validated by reengineering teams
• Visible to and supported by stakeholders

MONITORING THE TRANSFORMATION

Absolutely solid project management is required in change projects. Whether you are implementing limited or wide-scale change, the process will be complex. Monitoring and measuring progress in implementation will be just as difficult. This is where the rubber meets the road. Monitoring the transition provides you with information to:

• Determine whether desired benefits and improvements are being achieved.
• Flag potential problems arising from the transition.
• Keep the change project on schedule, on budget, and on course.
• Provide feedback to stakeholders, who need to remain "in the know" and to be reassured that the organization is progressing toward its performance improvement targets. As in all community endeavors, you must continuously assure change participants that their hard work is paying off.

WHEN BAD THINGS HAPPEN TO GOOD PROJECTS

Broad-based change projects are complex, therefore much can go wrong, and some things *will* go wrong under the sunniest of scenarios, if only due to Murphy's Law. Don't let that deter you. The chapters that follow are replete with solutions for overcoming the barriers to change, the setbacks you will assuredly encounter.

To give you some advance sense of common pitfalls to avoid, we discuss briefly below some of the bad things that can happen to good projects. Keep this list close by—we often hang it on the project war room wall as a caution to the project team.

1. Failure to deliver early, tangible results. Some would say the half-life of a change project is six months; that is, if you are not showing measurable results in six months, expect your support to halve and the barriers to double. On the whole, we endorse this observation. Obviously, six months is not the half-life of an ambitious project, but it may be the half-life of the support you initially receive. The worst thing you can do is design changes that require a huge investment and a long delivery time but offer no evidence of improved performance until a "big bang" implementation when the mayor cuts a ribbon and the trolleys start running. Would you seriously support such an effort? Would you fund it? Pressure the team to come up with a generous handful of near-term wins. Publicize those wins upon arrival to build momentum and support. A few quick, adequately dramatic wins will also reassure those who are funding your effort.

> **Even when breakthroughs are achieved on the conceptual level, implementation can be daunting.**

The need for quick results is real if for no other reason than to keep hope alive. The discomfort of change eventually touches all involved and, as it does, you can expect your change initiatives to encounter resistance. When the discomfort reaches a stakeholder group, hope can be replaced with skepticism, agreement with cynicism as to whether the changes can or even should be achieved. You will need to watch for this attitude; left unchallenged and uncorrected, it can spread and eliminate all hope of achieving what you have in mind. The material in Chapter Three on motivating stakeholders will help.

2. Talking about breakthroughs, drowning in detail. We have all heard the rhetoric about breakthroughs. While people often get excited about breakthrough possibilities at conferences, converting this excitement into sustained action back at the office on Monday morning is difficult. Even when breakthroughs are achieved on the conceptual level, implementation can be daunting. Yet breakthroughs are needed.

In many of the case studies in this book, breakthroughs are achieved *by simplifying rather than complicating* the way an organization operates. A simpler understanding of a problem and its solution, coupled with a sense of urgency to institute the simpler way quickly, can provide the breakthroughs for which so many companies are hungry. Detailed analysis and justification are probably necessary—this is the way of the world, or at least of our American corporate world—but meticulous documentation, complete with overheads, must not be permitted to obscure or derail what is probably a step toward simplicity and an authentic breakthrough.

A large gas company pursuing a project to uncover and cure problems in its gas accounting systems ultimately had to admit that the project had delivered little benefit. In the words of one executive: "The project team generated 180 feet of brown paper, and not much else." Symptomatic of overemphasis on process mapping (and underemphasis on practical, results-oriented change), the team had mapped business processes until both the team and its organizational sponsors were exhausted. The process review had yielded no real change or performance improvement. The team decided to stow most of its brown paper and start over—this time focusing on the highest-priority problems. And it is meeting with success in a project now guided by a considered look at that very powerful lever of change, the company's performance measures (see Chapter Nine).

3. Everything is high priority. Everything cannot be equally important. Life is full of choices. Change teams have to make them, too. Set a broad scope, and work for a while at that gauge, but then narrow in on the environment richest in targets. Pareto's Law (the 80-20 rule) is an Immutable Truth. Projects fail when priorities are not established early and refined *throughout* the effort.

4. Old performance measures block change. Fancy words cannot improve on the well-known assertion: "What gets measured, gets done." All large-scale change efforts demand a reshaping of the performance measures that guide manager and employee actions. If the long-established measures are not disassembled, they will continue to drive behavior and block the changes you have in mind. Think about the measures in your organization that really drive the actions and affect the attitudes of employees. Is behavior likely to change if they are not reshaped? Few policies are more effective in focusing employees' energies and attention than a properly designed performance management system. When your

measures are aligned with corporate strategies and goals, then your ability to drive change is greatly enhanced. Chapter Nine is dedicated to performance measures.

5. Failing to "connect the dots." Ideas compete in business just as they do on the field of battle and in politics. Business journals are rich in competing management techniques to improve business performance. While there are no pat solutions, many techniques (reengineering, TQM, and the like) are legitimate; they should be tuned to your organizational needs and put to work. However, failure to reconcile and integrate competing projects shaped by these methodologies can waste millions and exhaust your organization.

The energy and loyalty of good people pitted against one another in efforts to protect turf or programs is largely wasted, and the disruption from strenuous battles of this kind can be so thoroughgoing that no single project delivers on its promise. Chapter Six sheds, we believe, the necessary light on how to connect the dots for your employees; that is, how to harmonize and rationalize all of the legitimate change efforts under way in your organization.

6. The voice of the customer is absent. What influence has the customer on your change process? The customer is typically a consistent voice—and votes for what he values when he buys goods and services and pays the bill. The concept of systematically listening to the customer is fundamental in qualifying for the Baldrige Award in the United States and in qualifying to be examined for certification under ISO 9000 (the global quality standard). But long before the advents of total quality management, reengineering, and the Baldrige Award, an organization's skill in listening to the customer and translating customer needs into action went a long way toward explaining why businesses succeeded or failed. While this is a fundamental concept, few organizations systematically assess what the customer really wants. The voice of the customer is loud and clear in virtually every successful change effort we encounter. We recommend that key customers and suppliers be invited, as possible and appropriate, to serve as liaisons on the change project team.

> **The energy and loyalty of good people pitted against one another in efforts to protect turf or programs is largely wasted, and the disruption from strenuous battles of this kind can be so thoroughgoing that no single project delivers on its promise.**

7. The voice of the employee is not heard, either. Winning in sports takes belief in your team's ability to execute and excel. Surely you have watched many major sporting events where a single play or at-bat changed the entire momentum of competition. Change is a competition between the need for change and the barriers that resist it. Winning in a change project requires belief that barriers can be overcome and the end result will be worth the price. And this belief must be widespread; if the manager in the dugout or pacing the sidelines in a headset *believes*, but half the players have lost hope, the outcome is predictable. To achieve important, enduring, positive change, employee involvement is essential. Involving employees is messy. Wouldn't it be easier to form a small team, figure out the answers, and tell everybody else? But involvement builds commitment and significantly increases the likelihood of a successful transformation.

If your company has one or more unions, consider inviting the officials from your local's union committee to participate on the team. These elected officials represent one of the largest constituencies in your company. Their contributions and buy-in to the creation and implementation of the change plan will work wonders toward achieving a successful outcome. Even if there is no union presence, you would do well to act as if there is by identifying department leaders and working with them to sound out a great range of employee concerns and wishes.

In one recent assignment, we cautioned *against* empowering in certain respects the branch managers of a bank. You can imagine everyone's reaction in these heady days of employee empowerment.

8. Senior management wants to help, but doesn't know how. Every text and speech on change describes "top management commitment" as essential. Many bankrupt attempts at change result from failed efforts to maintain a visible level of support from the top. Our own experience is that top management typically means well but sometimes sends the wrong signals—often in the context of empowering employees. A new environment of empowerment is envisioned, and everyone buys in. But more than a few executives cannot seem to let go. They destroy momentum by confusing the message about change. Their heads tell them "share authority and we'll all win," their emotions tell them "share authority and *I'll* lose." Chapters Four and Five address these key questions of communicating honestly and empowerment.

9. "What's in it for me" is unclear. People change when the case for change becomes a personal matter. Too many change programs are naively based on the premise that changes in employee behaviors will occur "for the good of the enterprise" or "for the benefit of future generations of employees." Unlikely to the vanishing point. An employee will change his or her behavior when management honestly promises to make things better and communicates persuasively that the coming change project is part of the solution for that individual. The values in play are financial rewards, self-esteem, recognition, job satisfaction, career growth, pride, and numerous other personal tangibles and intangibles. It's only human: When we can't see what's in it for us, we're unlikely to change.

10. Too much conventional wisdom. Successful change programs require a solid foundation in fact, and one company's facts will be quite different from another's. This means that exemplary solutions, even if they are reported in the most trusted business reviews, may not work for you. Your facts may be different. Conventional wisdom can kill. In one recent assignment, we cautioned *against* empowering in certain respects the branch managers of a bank. You can imagine everyone's reaction in these heady days of employee empowerment. In this case, we believed the facts would show that a carefully crafted decision-support system would yield much better judgments than relatively autonomous branch managers. A test was conducted in which empowered managers made significantly poorer decisions than a decision-support system. The system was subsequently piloted and implemented.

Better change means better facts, better judgment. Chapter Five discusses how to use empowerment powerfully, to the advantage of both your business strategy and your employees.

11. Same old horses, same old glue. Failure to form a talented, diverse team representing all stakeholders is a cause of failure that often shows up too late to fix. Change means abandoning the current way of thinking. Teams that effectively drive change need to be populated with known innovators, not with status quo types— new blood, but not naive; diverse in style and background, but ready to cooperate; brash, but not rash. Where conventional wisdom says "it cannot be done here," real change teams will come up with breakthroughs.

BEYOND THE BASICS

The basics in this chapter set the stage for the challenge of achieving Better Change. Because comprehensive change is complex, these concepts call for elaboration and the support of real-world examples. The Price Waterhouse Change Integration® team has gathered its collective experience and observations into the eight chapters that follow. The chapters will lead you on a tour of change from building the case (Chapter Two) and knowing your stakeholders (Chapter Three) to communicating honestly (Chapter Four). This opening triad of chapters is dominated by conceptual and communications issues. The next three chapters address the reshaping of the organization through empowering people (Chapter Five), harmonizing concurrent change projects (Chapter Six), and redrawing or erasing internal boundaries so that the results of change projects can flow through and reach the customer (Chapter Seven). Chapter Eight, on thinking big and acting new, characterizes a corporate culture in which change processes are no longer unfamiliar; they are increasingly the way the game is played, and played well. Our concluding Chapter Nine addresses the real force in an organization—its performance measures—that can drive the organization's willingness to change or inadvertently preserve status quo, however unsatisfactory that status quo may be.

Good reading.

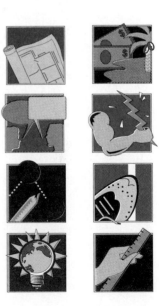

The organizational mechanisms of a termite hill, a beehive, or an ant colony seem fixed forever by nature. Defined by permanent roles in complex hierarchies, these social insects march forward through time doing, with immense industry, those things they are meant to do—and only those things. Our own business organizations are very different, much more flexible, ready to evolve as difficulties or opportunities signal the need for change. Or are they so different? This is a book about human organizations as they work toward their best, and their best is not fixed by nature. Their best is a dynamic balance between stability and change.

Admittedly, our organizations have something in common with the social insects: We don't reinvent everything everyday. On the other hand, when necessary, can we prove our fellowship with the caterpillar, which finds in its cocoon the blueprint—and the energy—for transformation?

The hardest thing about change is implementation. You have to start getting ready for implementation on the first day of your change project. More important still, you have to begin on day one to prepare your people for implementation.

Here's a diagnostic you can use as you are contemplating a change effort, or after evaluating your current environment, or even after designing your target environment as you are preparing for implementation. It is drawn from a one-day workshop used by Price Waterhouse to assess an organization's readiness for change, especially to:

- Raise the overall awareness of an organization regarding change, fundamentals of successfully managing the change process, and likely impacts.
- Surface hidden agendas and key resistance issues that might prove troublesome later if not discovered.
- Provide focus for later stages of the change effort.

Materials are available for performing this diagnostic in a workshop setting; see the business reply card at the back of this book for more information.

ACTIVITY 1:   ASSESSING LEVELS OF RESISTANCE TO CHANGE

It is human instinct to resist change. The following are examples of situations caused by a change effort that would lead to resistance to the change in yourself or others. You can perform this exercise using personal responses or an estimation of likely responses by others in your organization.

STEP 1:   If you believe that one of the following situations will be created as a result of your upcoming or current change effort, put a number next to it to indicate the degree of resistance that situation will engender (1 = low, 2 = medium, 3 = high).

____ Perceived threat to job security

____ Loss of expertise

____ Need to learn new skills

____ Shifts in influence, authority, control

____ Shifts in communication patterns

____ Loss of social status

____ Change in habits/customs

___ Limited understanding of the change and its implications

___ Low tolerance for change

___ **Total**

STEP 2: Total the numbers in the left-hand column. If your total is 10 or below, you have a manageable level of resistance. If your total is between 10 and 20, you need to make a special effort to deal with a significant level of resistance. If your total is 20 and above, you should stop any current change effort and reexamine your transition management plans to be sure that you are managing these serious levels of resistance.

STEP 3: Be sure to ask yourself:

What are the implications of these areas of expected resistance?

What can be done to mitigate the effects of resistance in these areas?

ACTIVITY 2: ASSESSING ABILITY TO MANAGE TRANSITIONS

This exercise points out various effective methods for managing transitions. The focus is on the importance of being proactive in managing transitions. Ten key fundamentals for successful, proactive transition management are listed below.

STEP 1: Review this list of 10 fundamentals, and then grade the effort (from A to F) being made in your current change project with respect to each fundamental.

Effort	Priority	Fundamental
_____	_____	**Leading.** Identifying and getting the support/commitment of key leaders within the organization undergoing the change.
_____	_____	**Visioning.** Articulating a clear, concise picture of how the organization will work and how it will be organized after the change is implemented.
_____	_____	**Assessing.** Determining the type and extent of impact the change will have on different dimensions of the organization; being proactive in defining and preparing for impacts rather than reactive to impacts after they occur.

Selling/marketing. Following common sales/marketing techniques in promoting the change and emphasizing the benefits.

Participating. Encouraging active involvement in creating and managing the change by all those directly or indirectly affected, as a means of building ownership.

Communicating. Exchanging regular and accurate information about the change in a proactive and open manner.

Educating. Providing training on the concepts and skills required to implement the change and to maximize effective work after the change.

Integrating. Coordinating the multiple activities and initiatives likely to be implemented as part of a major change.

Supporting. Confirming the infrastructure necessary to support the changes that will need to occur.

Transitioning. Preparing to move smoothly from the current environment to the target environment.

STEP 2:   After grading your project's performance in each of these fundamentals, rank the fundamentals in importance for your project using the following scale:

1 = high priority (no more than four of these)
2 = medium priority (no more than three of these)
3 = low priority

You may believe that all fundamentals are high priority, but if you establish relative importance, you can better decide how to allocate resources and time.

STEP 3:   Compare priority and effort grades. This will indicate where you need to pay more attention. For instance, any high-priority fundamental area with less than a B needs immediate attention, or the success of your current change effort will remain at risk.

ACTIVITY 3:   IDENTIFY AND PRIORITIZE KEY IMPACT AREAS

This exercise identifies areas within the organization that will be affected by the change process. Completing this impact assessment enables you to estimate how a particular change may affect various areas of the organization. This is a preliminary assessment. The goal is to flag potential impact areas so that action plans can be initiated and carefully monitored. You can reuse this tool as more specifics about the change are understood.

STEP 1: Based on your current change effort, designate whether the impact in that area is expected to be high (H), medium (M), or low (L). Designate no more than four high-impact areas and three medium-impact areas.

Impact	Priority	Impact Area
____	____	**Culture**. The basic values and beliefs of the organization.
____	____	**Organization structure**. The formal and informal structures used to organize the company, division, or department.
____	____	**Business processes**. The way in which business events are handled during day-to-day operations; how inputs are turned into outputs.
____	____	**Job design**. The roles, responsibilities, and authority assigned to specific jobs within the organization.
____	____	**Skills/knowledge required**. The special knowledge, skills, or capabilities required of the work force to perform their jobs effectively.
____	____	**Worker motivation**. The formal and informal rewards provided to the work force, the internal drives/motivations within the work force itself, and the extent to which these two correspond.
____	____	**Communications**. The formal and informal patterns of communication and information flow within the organization and the correspondence of these patterns to work force motivations.
____	____	**Operating policies**. Formal and informal guidelines for daily work activities; policies provide general guidelines while procedures define specific action requirements.
____	____	**Human resources management.** Administrative activities related to the

recruitment, selection, retention, and development of the work force.

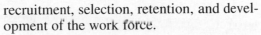 **Technology interfaces.** The required use of technology to perform job tasks and the amount/nature of the interfaces between users and technology.

STEP 2: After estimating the expected degree of impact in each of these areas, prioritize the list of impact areas based on whether successful change in each area is critical to the success of the overall change. Rank each area as:

1 = high priority (no more than four of these)
2 = medium priority (no more than three of these)
3 = low priority

You may believe that all impact areas are high priority, but if you establish relative importance, you can better decide how to allocate resources and time.

STEP 3: Compare impact areas and priorities. This will indicate where you need to pay more attention. For instance, any high-priority impact area where high or medium change impact is expected needs immediate attention, or the success of your current change effort will remain at risk.

In planning how to deal with these impact areas, estimate the type of impact and likely issues that will arise. Identify possible action steps for key areas of concern.

Building the Case for Change

I t's almost instinctive to think of change programs as an intensive kind of "doing," and that's not wrong. They require a lot of "doing" to get things right. But there is a demanding preliminary phase in successful change processes that we call building the case for change. It is less a doing than a conceptual challenge and a dialogue requiring some of your hardest-won management skills. In this phase, you form and share your vision with all stakeholders inside and outside of your organization; you demonstrate to all concerned the good sense, even the power of that vision; and you invite them to participate in concrete, creative ways. On the way to this communication of the case for change, you will need to analyze your stakeholder population because their stakes and motivations—and their power to resist, topple, or enhance your change program—are going to be very different from one another. You need to know where they are likely to stand so that you address each group's aspirations and fears with precision. This activity of building the case for change is not just a preliminary; the message needs to be reinforced as you go along. This is a chapter about all of these things, and the material here is of a make-or-break nature. Without properly building the case for change, there may be no meaningful change at the end of the day.

• • •

Imagine yourself a prosecuting attorney, a rising star. You're trying the case of your life. This is the one that may lead to national prominence, perhaps elected office. You're arguing the death penalty for a brutal criminal. You work endlessly to prepare an airtight case. No question about it, you deliver a flawless closing argument. All this, only to discover that a seemingly shy member of the jury has emerged as a lion—and he is adamantly opposed to capital punishment.

Do not assume for a moment that those whose jobs (and lives) will be changed by what you intend will conveniently and effortlessly buy in.

Didn't you present a compelling case? Wasn't the outcome you sought not merely lawful but just?

This vignette calls to mind a far more dramatic circumstance than the average corporate change program. But the frustrations we've witnessed in business leaders trying to convince others in their organizations of the need to change—and change now—are no less disheartening.

In our experience, the highest barrier to change is that the organization is often simply not ready for it. Accordingly, it is best to begin a change project with the realization that the case for change is not yet made. Do not assume for a moment that those whose jobs (and lives) will be changed by what you intend will conveniently and effortlessly buy in. Even those who appear to be in favor of change need to be convinced, for many of them will not understand the magnitude or the nature of change you may be contemplating. Alternatively, they may view change as "something *those folks* have to do."

WHAT IS A CASE FOR CHANGE?

A case for change is a reasoned yet powerfully persuasive justification for the changes targeted by your change effort. To be effective, your case for change should be:

- Brief
- Clear
- Well articulated
- Logical
- Qualitative *and* quantitative
- Well documented
- Compelling

Above all, *it must build a strong sense of urgency*. It must drive people to action.

No one had to persuade those on the *Titanic* to take action. They moved smartly to the lifeboats. But crises seldom come upon business organizations with the sudden impact of an iceberg in the fog-bound North Atlantic. Most crises build one month at a time.

Almost everyone in business has contemplated at some point the terrible fate of a certain frog. As the story goes, if you put a frog in a pot of boiling water, the shock is so great it will immediately jump out. The crisis is upon it, it acts. However, the story continues, if you put the frog in a pot of cool water and raise the temperature gradually, the frog will accept its circumstances and eventually expire as the water rises to the boiling point.

As ugly as this picture is to contemplate, isn't this what is happening in too many organizations today? Conditions worsen for all kinds of reasons that go unattended. Some organizations long ignore the danger signs foretelling the need for change. Finally, after years of deteriorating performance—when the water has reached 140 degrees fahrenheit and can no longer be mistaken for a hot tub—everyone begins to feel the heat and recognizes that there *must* be change.

That may be a blessing of sorts—at least for the person wanting to drive change. Larry Bossidy, a CEO who has had a major impact at AlliedSignal, believes his successful change programs have benefited from the fact that his people fully recognized that change—significant change—was necessary. He credits some of his ability to effect substantial change at AlliedSignal to the relative ease with which it was possible to develop the case for change.

DOESN'T THE CASE FOR CHANGE SPEAK FOR ITSELF?

Earlier in this decade, many organizations—swollen with staff beyond levels they could sustain and with profits decaying—announced large-scale "restructurings." Few days went by in which we weren't informed of another giant corporation planning to lay off tens of thousands of workers. Most of this activity was the clear result of major profit problems facing these organizations. And declining profitability was in turn a function of increasing global competition and of faltering economies around the world.

But something new started to occur in 1993. Press reports began heralding the downsizing of companies *without* profit problems. Organizations assumed by the public to be weathering these storms quite nicely began to restructure, and their CEOs were regularly quoted to the effect that their companies *must* change—for example, they *must* ready themselves both for increased pricing pressures in their traditional markets and to facilitate their entry into new markets (Russia, China, etc.) with basic, low-cost products. All of this may have seemed natural to you as a regular reader of the business news. But many people will express surprise when hugely successful companies declare the need for dramatic change affecting the lives of thousands of employees. Public reaction to those reports is a manifestation of the general naiveté regarding the need for change. People are shocked. They can't conceive of *successful* companies embarking upon radical change. Take this into consideration if your company is not in crisis. The declaration of a major change program—the case for change—needs to be made persuasively even by companies with room to maneuver and a strong history of profits.

> **Surprisingly, people at the "bottom" of the organization usually resist least, because they know how bad things really are and they are willing to try almost anything to improve the situation.**

As a change agent, you need to measure the receptivity of your organization to the kind and scope of change you have in mind. Be conservative in this initial assessment. If, as you communicate the case for change, you find yourself preaching to the choir, so much the better. The alternative is ugly: discovering late in the game that your detailed plans for change—prepared with great effort by you and your team—are being blocked or sidetracked because powerful stakeholder groups are not even convinced of the need to change, let alone of the virtues of your plans.

GAUGING THE NEED; MONITORING EFFECTIVENESS

Gauging the need for building the case for change will help you better know the task ahead. You will also gain insight into the perceptions of individual stakeholders. The "change readiness" material at the end of Chapter One provides you with a good cross section of questions and issues to explore in determining just how robust a case must be developed. Consider conducting a change readiness workshop. It will be most revealing.

Once you begin to communicate the case for change, you can measure how well you are doing by the frequency and enthusiasm with which people sign up. Are the best people in your organization falling over themselves to become part of the team? Or are you spending what comes to seem far too much time recruiting—and eliciting only a lukewarm response? You'll be oversubscribed only if your stakeholders understand and believe in the need for change.

CHANGE WHAT?

When we survey employees during a change project, it is not uncommon to find that their expectations about what will change vary significantly. Many envision new technologies dominating the improvement effort; others focus on changes in process or business practices; some perceive organizational change. Very few, however, perceive change in multiple facets of the organization (process, technology, people, culture, organization); they commonly recognize change in no more than one or two dimensions. Part of preparing them—and yourself—for what's ahead is letting them know the scope of change to be expected. If they are not expecting change in the organizational structure, for example, they may not initially resist. However, as organizational changes they have not been helped to anticipate begin to unfold, you may encounter much more resistance than you expected—and it may derail you. Know what you're up against. Communicate candidly what's ahead.

SEGMENT THE STAKEHOLDERS

As the change sponsor, you must recognize the differences in view held by the various stakeholder groups. For example, people at different levels of the organization resist change for different reasons.

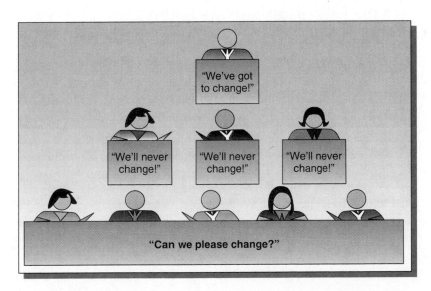

FIGURE 2.1
STAKEHOLDER
PERCEPTIONS AT
DIFFERENT LEVELS.

Surprisingly, people at the "bottom" of the organization usually resist least, because they know how bad things really are and they are willing to try almost anything to improve the situation. Typically, the greatest resistance to change comes from middle managers, whose resistance issues tend to focus on loss of power or the risk of failure. Their classic strategy for fighting loss of turf (or, as they fear, their jobs) is to stonewall change.

Stakeholder segmentation should be detailed enough to allow you to shape a focused communications campaign to move them toward your objectives. The message you want to get to "the folks in accounting" is likely to be different from (but not inconsistent with) the communiqué to plant managers.

BE CREATIVE IN BUILDING YOUR CASE

Everyone in business is aware of the information overload—and no one can really keep up. As you make the case for change, you will face that overload as other people experience it, and you will need to overcome it. If your message is to get through to influential stakeholders, it needs the best creative thinking you and your team can bring to it.

One of the most creative cases for change we have observed mobilized support for a major overhaul of procurement processes at a large restaurant chain. The initial situation was not especially promising. The change sponsor was simply unable to get management excited about the need to redesign the procurement processes (including the supporting technology, organization, etc.). Yet he knew how badly change was needed and how much opportunity for improvement existed. He needed senior management's attention in the worst way.

He decided to make a low-budget video to document the inefficiency of current processes and the crying need for change. Off he went, armed with his own video camera. His cinema verité production was not a work of art, but it *worked*. To depict the entire supply chain, his documentary began with a shot of a patch of dirt (lettuce—just after being planted!) and ended with a customer chowing down a cheeseburger (lettuce and all).

Art it wasn't. High impact it was. It did a wonderful job of illustrating how clumsy the current processes were.

He sent a copy of the video to each senior executive. Their response was predictable. His imaginatively packaged case for change hit the mark. From that point forward, the project was on everybody's radar screen.

CHAPTER TWO

HELP YOUR ORGANIZATION VISUALIZE CHANGE

Your creative efforts will have to extend to helping stakeholders visualize the changes you're contemplating. One change sponsor we know was leading an effort to improve the design of the retail outlets at his company. Over a weekend, he and his team cut up and taped together cardboard boxes to represent various store configurations, simulating new in-store designs and activities as they envisioned them. Their "stage set" was the floor of an empty warehouse. When they were ready, they invited key stakeholders to their little diorama—to great effect. Their audience could now grasp the nature of the changes being considered. With greater understanding came dialogue and, eventually, support for the project ahead.

> **Often the best shock-wave communiqué is some truth that's gone unsaid—some fact, known to most everyone, but never openly faced before for any number of reasons.**

UNDERSTANDING THEIR STAKES

The people in your organization need to understand their stakes in the change program. Nothing more effectively motivates them to play an active, positive role in the effort. Perhaps most important, they need to understand that the improvements you have in mind are the basis for *continuous change*—and they have a role to play in that, as well. A strong case for change is a motivator but, unfortunately, many organizations do not clearly understand this. Instead, they concentrate on building an unimpeachable statement of purpose that somehow leaves people out and gives stakeholders little sense of their role, their risks, their opportunities. "This is what is going to happen and why." Not good enough. The case for change must be a call to arms.

TELL THE TRUTH

Strangely enough, the truth is often a powerful pill. Employees today are so hardened and skeptical that you have to send a message that resonates with them. Often the best shock-wave communiqué is some truth that's gone unsaid—some fact, known to most everyone, but never openly faced before for any number of reasons. We were present, for example, when the CEO of a company with a long tradition of success declared that the strategy of a major division had failed. It was true. Everybody knew it. But people were still shaken by the message—shaken and relieved. The issues were finally being faced. It was OK to face them. Things at last were going to change.

PROVIDE DIRECTION; ENCOURAGE DISCOVERY

An effective case for change joins a clear and persuasive vision of strategic direction with specific supporting actions. But not all the actions need to be, can be, or should be detailed. The fact that you do not know how every single detail will work out leaves an important opening for stakeholder discovery. The best case for change, then, is built on two values: direction and discovery.

• *Direction* establishes a destination and a plan for getting there.
• *Discovery* is your explicit invitation to stakeholders to participate as creative agents in the change process rather than to apply the brakes or position themselves as victims.

Too often the case for change places all the weight on the first value only. The change sponsor establishes a clear vision, and people understand it—as far as it goes. But the sponsor fails to show clearly, even dramatically, that this is their program, too, and they can influence it in substantive, positive ways. You must earn stakeholder buy-in, and the invitation to discovery has proven earning power.

TUNE YOUR CASE TO KEY STAKEHOLDERS

The way in which you present the case for change needs to be attuned to the needs and views of the various stakeholders you have identified. For example, the case as presented internally will almost certainly differ from the case as presented to external stakeholders. In some instances, those outside your organization can emerge as key influences on your success—or failure. But one trait is virtually certain to be common to all your presentations: the need to overcome the self-limiting ideas of your stakeholders. You will have to demonstrate that a real paradigm shift is occurring—that familiar answers referencing "company policy" or "lack of resources" no longer have a place in the organization, that what you plan is not just possible but imminent and real.

You will have to demonstrate that a real paradigm shift is occurring—that familiar answers referencing "company policy" or "lack of resources" no longer have a place in the organization, that what you plan is not just possible but imminent and real.

Here is how a multinational retailer handled a key external stakeholder group.

BUILDING A CASE FOR CHANGE WITH SUPPLIERS

The Latin American operation of a US-based multinational retailer decided to use electronic data interchange (EDI) to reengineer its procurement processes to stay competitive both in its domestic market and in the global arena. The idea was to establish a "quick response" system for replenishing merchandise. Sensible as this goal surely was, it made the retailer's local trading partners anxious. EDI was not a new concept; they were well aware of it, and most of them understood the potential benefits. However, their nation's telecommunications infrastructure was not comparable to that of the United States, and they were worried that EDI technology would demand too much of it. In addition, many believed that migrating to advanced procurement techniques could be too much for their organizations. Something to do in time, yes—but not so quickly.

An impasse? No. The solution was to work with these partners from the beginning and to sell them on the feasibility and benefits of the new technology. Seminars were specially organized to educate their key managers. One-on-one meetings were organized so technical and line representatives of the retailer could meet their counterparts from the supplier companies and engage in "discovery" dialogue. Everyone was encouraged to have a voice, to participate.

The retailer built and communicated a compelling case for change based on logic, economics, and external benchmarks, that is, a well-documented overview of what other retailer/supplier networks were doing. The fear factor was turned into a motivator as well. After listening and questioning, suppliers had to ask themselves: "What if I *don't* change? Where will I be in two years?"

After securing the buy-in of a majority of its suppliers and implementing the system, the retailer found—as its studies had indicated—that international standards of EDI were easily adaptable to this nation's business environment and telecommunications infrastructure. Within a year, the retailer was showing a positive return on its investment in the new system.

BENCHMARKING FOR COMPETITIVE CONTEXT

Benchmarking the practices or performance of your organization against those of peers is a powerful means of developing your case for change. By measuring "best-in-class" performance, your

FIGURE 2.2
REPORTING OF
BENCHMARKING
(EXAMPLE)

Intelligent external benchmarking can provide you with important insights regarding opportunities for improvement. It also provides a strong component for your case for change.

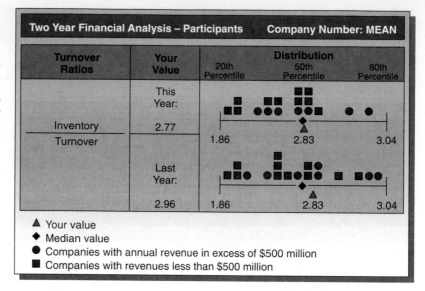

| Two Year Financial Analysis – Participants | | Company Number: MEAN | | |

Turnover Ratios	Your Value	Distribution 20th Percentile	50th Percentile	80th Percentile
Inventory Turnover	This Year: 2.77	1.86	2.83	3.04
	Last Year: 2.96	1.86	2.83	3.04

▲ Your value
◆ Median value
● Companies with annual revenue in excess of $500 million
■ Companies with revenues less than $500 million

benchmarking research can convert a merely plausible case for change into a call to arms. What may have seemed to some stakeholders merely an internal issue to be pursued at a convenient pace or not at all may suddenly acquire urgency as a matter of competitive survival; hence, the interest in and importance of benchmarking.

As benchmarking's value in building the case for change has become more widely recognized as a need-to-have rather than a nice-to-have, the sophistication and utility of benchmarking have grown substantially. Today, it is no longer enough to collect a few external productivity statistics and ensure that they are sufficiently relevant to your operations to justify direct comparison. To support a sustainable case for change, a balanced and complete benchmarking effort in many instances will consider all the following factors:

• **Process/performance benchmarks**. The classic staple of benchmarking is the measured results (known as metrics) achieved by competitors or world-class performers in various processes *and* the methods used to achieve those results. We make it a practice to organize the benchmark information in a way that highlights the levers of management control: process, people, structure, and technology.

• **Strategic/competitive benchmarks**. The direction for a change initiative may involve shifts in competitive strategy. Where this is so, the benchmark set should include information on the markets and products/services of competitors.

CHAPTER TWO

• **Customer/supplier benchmarks**. Factual, current information on the expectations and needs of customers, and how they match the capabilities, priorities, and image of your operations, is central to building a sustainable case for change. Likewise, credible and fresh information on the nature and extent of supplier partnerships among your leading competitors is necessary to round out the case for change.

• **Work force benchmarks**. Building a sustainable case for change requires an honest assessment of the organization's readiness and capacity for change. It is not enough to declare your commitment to an empowered work force; any such commitment must reflect full consideration of the appropriate levels of empowerment at different levels of your operations and the skills and capabilities of your current work force.

SUSTAINING THE CASE FOR CHANGE

How do you get them moving and keep them moving? Let's look for a moment at the experiences of two companies with a similar problem—the need to improve order management—and how these organizations were affected by the way the respective cases (on the following pages) for change were built.

This case study sounds straightforward, and it is. Unfortunately, not every organization goes down a comparable path.

SAY IT AGAIN, SAM

Your urgent message, unfortunately, will have only passing significance to your audience unless you deliver it often. The communications wisdom of the world all points in the same direction. Advertising executives will tell you that if you don't insert an ad—the same ad—at least three times in a publication, you might as well not invest in advertising. The maxim of effective preachers is to "tell them what you're going to say, say it, and then tell them what you've said." Fortunately, even if the core message remains the same, the details of your case for change will alter over time as the implementation begins to deliver results and surfaces new possibilities. You need to stay fresh in front of the communications task,

> By measuring "best-in-class" performance, your benchmarking research can convert a merely plausible case for change into a call to arms.

without overlooking the fact that repetition is the point. Too much is riding on a major change project to let any stakeholder stand in its way unnecessarily.

BUILDING A STRONG CASE UP AND DOWN THE ORGANIZATION

An office products manufacturer was taking too long to fill orders and, as a result, was losing customers. Financial results were falling short of projections for key indicators such as return on operating revenues. The company was not adapting to major changes in the industry. For example, discount merchandisers and office product superstores were transforming the traditional distribution channels that had once been dominated by wholesalers and retail outlets. This transformation was squeezing margins throughout the industry and putting pressure on manufacturers to shrink order fulfillment cycle times from days or weeks to hours and eliminating back orders as an accepted practice. On top of this, new manufacturers were outperforming the established players in terms of their responsiveness to customers, ability to fill complete orders, and use of technologies favored by mass merchandisers, such as electronic data interchange.

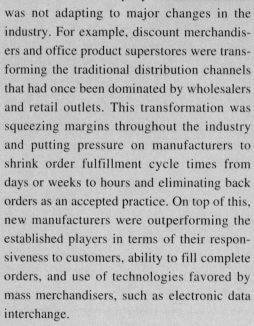

This manufacturer's first reaction was to purchase a new order management system in an attempt to speed up order processing. The company prepared a strategic systems plan and purchased a new software package. The intent was to automate the current process. It also began to use EDI for a small percentage of orders from selected large customers that demanded it.

One year after the order management software purchase, the software still sat in the shrink-wrap waiting to be implemented and the use of EDI was still a very small percent of total orders. The few EDI orders that were received were printed out and handled manually. No one had a vision of how the order process needed to change to improve performance. They didn't really know what was wrong with their existing process, except that it didn't work well. In this situation, users and MIS could not finalize requirements and begin implementing the software.

THE PERSUASIVE POWER OF ACTION

The case for change cannot be built on the classic bromides. Simply describing the benefits of more and better systems, training, strategy, and communication will not necessarily be effective in changing the organization. These familiar solutions need to be

The director of Order Management Services decided to take action. He realized he would have to reengineer the processes under his control, but he knew that building a persuasive case for change came first. He began by mapping the work flows in his department to identify opportunities to improve cycle times and reduce errors, and he found widespread evidence of significant non-value-added activities. When he presented the findings to upper managers, they were shocked and promptly accepted the need for dramatic improvements. They empowered the director and his staff to begin reengineering.

To build the case for change among other key stakeholders (order processors, customer service representatives, sales and marketing, et al.), the director of Order Management followed a very important rule: Get as many people involved in the process as you can. He wanted at least 10 percent of the affected employees in key stakeholder groups to be actively involved in teams established to rethink the current process and figure out how to do it better. A small group closeted in a back room might have been faster and might have produced a tighter solution, but then failed to sell "their" ideas to those who had to accept them.

To avoid the us versus them phenomenon, the company used its existing TQM framework to form teams, conduct meetings, and communicate. The result was that key stakeholders participated, saw for themselves what needed to change, and ended up convincing each other of the need for change in the course of the natural give and take required to find a solution to the problems in order management. This approach to change made the stakeholders more receptive to the truth about the company's competitive position, the increasingly more stringent demands of customers, and inefficiencies in the current process.

Within a year, the company had reduced the work steps required to process an order by 40 percent, eliminated archival filing, and increased the volume of orders accepted electronically by a multiple of 12. Late in 1993, it selected *new* order management software (the original package was found not to meet requirements) and is currently implementing a system that supports the new work flows and the revised order management organizational structure.

woven together into a pattern of aggressive actions, convincing those in your organization that the train is leaving the station. They have a choice: They can get on the train or they can miss the train. A powerful case for change will have them scrambling for seats in the station.

PERILS OF PROMOTION

After the merger of a large petroleum products distributor with a similar organization, the need for change in many dimensions of the resulting organization was apparent to senior management. They focused on the need to integrate and improve two very different order management systems—in a word, to reengineer the merged system. The overriding goal was improved customer service. A reengineering team was appointed. It promptly undertook site visits to benchmark the existing system against other companies perceived to have "world-class" order management processing. The team worked hard, and in due course it produced an exciting yet well-detailed vision. The reengineered process promised an *80 percent reduction in lead times* and other benefits as well. The team was sold. Enthusiasm was high.

Now, how was everyone else feeling?

The team's successful efforts generated an unexpected result. Thanks in part to his good efforts in the process redesign, the project sponsor was promoted to a new position. After this move, the reengineering project lost momentum, suffered a funding cut when the company hit a bad patch, and languished, unimplemented, more than a year later.

Why wasn't the new system implemented? The problem it was meant to address didn't go away: Customers remained less happy than they might be. But those who were now accountable for processing orders did not share the change sponsor's vision—*and never had really shared it.*

For a change project to outlive its original sponsor, the case for change must be established in a way that identifies and addresses every constituency affected by the project. It must create an environment that demands change, and it must pull change irresistibly forward. Our account of the early stages of this reengineering project makes no mention of "going public" with the rationale for change, of an organized communications effort relating to specific stakeholder groups. The project leader did personally evangelize, but the inadequacy of that approach was now apparent: With his departure, no one else really cared, no one stepped forward as an effective sponsor.

WALK THE TALK

Once your change program is under way, actions will speak loudly. Many people in your organization will become true believers only when they see the benefits of change begin to accrue. Actions that counter limiting ideas and support the change initiative build the integrity and credibility of your case for change.

"Up and Down" versus "Perils"

Consider the differences between change management at the office products manufacturer in the first case study and change management at the petroleum products distributor. The key difference lies in the strength of the case for change and its initial presentation, which laid the foundation for ownership by other stakeholders. In the first company, an evenly paced educational and participatory process created internal demand for reengineering. The change team addressed separate stakeholder groups and entered into individual dialogue with key managers. As a result, whole groups understood the value of the project and influential executives *wanted* to be involved in the change project; they lined up to have their piece of the implementation. It did not hurt, of course, that the president expressed solid support and frequently praised the project in meetings and newsletters.

What began as a systems upgrade at the office products manufacturer soon evolved into a reengineering of the entire order management function—with the participation and consent of employees who were now confident that the old ways of doing their jobs would not be senselessly obliterated. They were among the architects of change.

The Information Services Department (the change sponsor) was delighted to have users united behind a set of requirements. Even the head of Customer Service stepped forward to promote the reengineering effort—publicly admitting, with some chagrin, that the number of non-value-added tasks embedded in the old process was excessive.

Throughout the effort, the case for change was reinforced and grew stronger. Managers and supervisors in Order Management sponsored improvement teams of their own. Order Management employees understood customer needs and offered valuable suggestions for improvements. When the founding sponsors of parts of the change program moved on, new leaders were waiting in the wings to make it happen.

Taking it as a given that the change programs at both the office products company and the petroleum products distributor were totally valid, full of benefits for their companies, what we have measured here is the importance of making the case for change effectively.

REFRESHING YOUR CASE

The case must be continually renewed. Look at what happened at the music division of one of the world's largest entertainment companies, where a merger of business units prompted the reengineering of the procurement and disbursement processes.

CASE STUDY

SUSTAIN THE CASE FOR CHANGE

A large media and entertainment multinational had grown through the acquisition of several smaller companies. Everyone agreed it was time to coordinate the back office operations of the former businesses into one strong unit for the merged operation. Executive management had an ambitious reengineering agenda: world-class operation, breakthrough performance improvement, low-cost delivery of transaction processing services.

The vision set by management was to achieve a paperless "requisition-to-check" processing environment with reductions in invoice process cycle times from 6.5 weeks to 1 week and a 90 percent reduction in invoice tracking effort. However—and this is the key environmental factor—the case for change was *not* driven by immediate competitive problems or imminent threat of operational failure. Consequently, senior executive attention to the project was expected to fluctuate, and the change team gave much thought to a strategy for sustaining management commitment—and the team's own momentum. The resulting strategy shows the value of going the extra mile or two. The fully elaborated change plan included not only a bold, leading-edge vision but also a demonstration of the value of the vision through a prototype software application—in effect, a sample implementation. The prototype demonstrated dramatic benefits and handily reinforced management's commitment to the changes.

Where the case for change is not driven by immediate and pressing difficulties, it is key to sustain management commitment through a demonstration of value. Further, the case for change needs to be constantly reinforced and refreshed throughout the change process. Change teams that fail to communicate effectively as they go along put their project at risk.

What can be said generally about building the case for change ends here. The next move, naturally, is yours. Your own circumstances, your own scenarios will necessarily differ from any we have discussed, but experience indicates that the basic principles apply. The challenge is many-sided: not just process analysis but vision, not just broadband communication but segmented and focused communication, not just consensus building at the beginning but consensus building throughout.

___ Tell the truth. Begin making the case for change with utter candor, and keep on telling the truth. This is your most powerful tool.

___ Build and communicate a powerful and compelling case for change by being:

___ Brief	___ Well articulated
___ Clear	___ Qualitative and quantitative
___ Logical	___ Prepared with the facts
___ Compelling	___ Well documented

___ Be creative to get attention and to be heard, heeded, and supported. Create a two- or three-dimensional picture of the change and its benefits in your stakeholders' minds.

___ Tune the message appropriately for different stakeholder groups: inside versus outside the company, management versus staff, resister versus change agent.

___ When you don't have a crisis to make your case, focus on a demonstration of value and benefits to be gained through change. Companies with spotless reputations and room to maneuver must be the most persuasive to convince stakeholders of the need for proactive change.

___ Measure readiness for change and build your case accordingly. (The change readiness material at the end of Chapter One will help.)

___ Communicate candidly what's ahead. This enables you to surface and mitigate resistance before it derails your implementation.

___ Link stakeholder wins to your change program. Look for common goals; be specific.

___ Once you've established and communicated each stakeholder's benefits, show them how they can participate in the change.

___ Make this participation substantive; stakeholders must help design and implement the change to own it.

___ Give each a role not only in the change project, but also in the ongoing continuous improvement effort.

___ Use benchmarking to garner the facts and context needed to create a sense of urgency in your case for change.

___ Beware of complacency when you have a strong mandate for change. Repeat and refresh the message or risk its being lost—along with the mandate—in the welter of day-to-day business.

THREE

Motivating Stakeholders

The concept of stakeholders has not always been with us. It has gained currency in the past decade or so as business leaders have more acutely recognized the complex web of relationships that make possible their organizations' success. It is a democratic concept growing out of a pragmatic regard for diversity. And it is a key concept for those who sponsor major change. You will need to meet stakeholders where they are, inside and outside the organization, and you will need to invite them persuasively to join you where you are: at the cutting edge of change and good fortune for your company.

• • •

You've seen them—up on the stage, strutting back and forth, delivering a fast-paced message of inspiration, hope, enthusiasm, encouragement. In the end, you can't help yourself—you're pumped up, excited, ready to take on the world. Their goal is to motivate, to incite you to act anew—to change. Roger Staubach, Lou Holtz, Norman Vincent Peale come to mind. The motivational speaker is an American icon that will be with us for a long time. These people look as if they're having fun up there on the stage, and they probably are. You can, too.

We are not going to suggest you work up a heart-thumping speech to deliver to those who have stakes in the changes you're contemplating. But you do need to begin to think about how, *in your own way*, you can bring them on board to support change. Experience shows that this is a major hurdle standing between your change project on paper and your change project as an implemented reality. Nothing is less impressive than a change project that doesn't reach its stakeholders—a flat tire comes to mind. All of the big ideas in the world go nowhere if the people affected by and affecting them do not give projects the support they need.

Motivating stakeholders to make your agenda theirs is no easy task. One reason for its difficulty is that so many stakeholders are involved in complex change. Start with everyone inside your organization affected by and capable of influencing the change process, then move on to everyone who comes in contact with your organization. Adding to the complexity, stakeholding individuals and groups perceive themselves as having different stakes. Further, their views of how things are going and what it all means are certain to evolve in the course of the project—implying that you will need periodically to revisit stakeholders to hear their hopes and fears and to reinstill the positive change message. Finally, the greatest obstacle to successful change may be your organization's past experience with change. That experience is surely mixed at best, and whatever was nasty or difficult about it will have left some key stakeholders fearful, cynical, even angry.

Because stakeholders differ in perspective, we recommend that you identify an initial set of stakeholding individuals and groups and take steps to understand how they view the changes ahead. Further, you will need to continue to identify new players as they enter the game and monitor their emerging enthusiasm and concerns. And you will have to do something about the baggage each stakeholder brings on this journey.

WHO ARE THESE STAKEHOLDERS?

Stakeholders are individuals or groups who, at some time during the change cycle, will affect and be affected by what is happening. Obvious stakeholders are those directly involved in the changes. How much farther you should look for stakeholders depends on the scope of your effort and its objectives. As we noted above, when broad-based change is at issue the full stakeholder population frequently includes individuals or groups outside the organization. Stakeholders include:

• **Customers.** You must have noticed that customers always come first? More than any other factor, customers help focus your efforts by telling you what they need—and just as important, what they don't need. When these things become your focus, you can eliminate vast amounts of time spent on activities they don't value. Amazing though it seems, in almost every process reengineering assignment in which we have helped client teams analyze and assess the activities underlying their fundamental business processes, little more than a quarter of these activities add value in the eyes of the customer. Think of it: 75 percent or more of the activity, energy, and money expended does *not* contribute to the creation of value—the purpose for which your organization exists. Make it your objective to harness more of that energy to activities customers pay for. There is tremendous leverage here, if you succeed.

• **Employees.** Employee groups usually come first to mind when one thinks of stakeholders in a broad-based organizational change effort. As you begin to envision change, you will find yourself asking questions like these: Will the folks in operations go along with this? Will the sales force feel threatened by these changes? How can we get Corporate MIS to support my plan to have our own system at the plant? You will also find yourself thinking about individuals: Will Bob Delaney see this as a threat? How will Sheila McIntyre react? As you identify the various stakeholders with whom you need to work, you will inevitably build a list of influential groups *and* individuals.

The greatest obstacle to successful change may be your organization's past experience with change. That experience is surely mixed at best, and whatever was nasty or difficult about it will have left some key stakeholders fearful, cynical, even angry.

• **Owners.** Naturally, you won't want to ignore the company's owners and shareholders. They have invested in the organization; their interest in its success is paramount. As you move through the change process, it will remain a good idea to keep the members of this group high on your radar screen—not that they will be looking over your shoulder (seldom the case), but keeping their interests in mind and picking up dialogue with them at key points will help you focus on what is best for the enterprise as a whole and keep you focused on a balanced view of priorities. In one of our recent projects, in which there were many tough interdepartmental issues to resolve, the project director hung a huge sign in the project war room that read, *"Ask yourself what the owners want."* It was a healthy reminder.

• **Suppliers and other business partners.** Consider suppliers and strategic business partners in your stakeholder plans—external allies can be useful. Consistent with the trend toward reducing sources and developing supplier quality programs, your organization is probably working with fewer suppliers. These vendors are likely to know your business well, and they should be willing to invest time and resources in your success. The good ones care about your performance because they recognize that their success depends on your success. Consider how they can help you effect the change you're after. For example, most suppliers know, up to a point, what your competitors are doing. Drawing sensibly on this information—we're not proposing industrial espionage—can provide you with interesting external perspectives and valuable competitive benchmarks.

The more stakeholders feel involved in assessing the need for change and in shaping the nature of change, the more prepared they will be to commit to change and contribute to its success. This is buy-in.

• **You and your team.** Your interest in change is real. If you are a member of the core team driving change, your stake in the success of the effort is significant. Strange as it may seem, we suggest you monitor formally *your own* stake in these changes. How will the changes impact you and your team? In the interest of candor, get it down on paper.

KNOW THY STAKEHOLDERS

The more specifically you know your stakeholder groups and individuals, the better you'll be able to foresee how to influence them. To develop an effective plan, you will need to consider each one, if necessary subdividing them into smaller groups or identifying key individuals within groups, so that you have a credible map of their perceived interests and levels of influence. You will then need to shape and document a specific action plan detailing how you intend to bring each constituency on board. The two key questions on people's minds are likely to be these:

1. **How will this affect me?** This is first and foremost. Stakeholders will be evaluating the change project in terms of their own potential wins and real or feared losses. Conjecture on your part is dangerous; change leaders, however perceptive, seldom guess correctly how stakeholders perceive forthcoming changes. It is best to ask.

2. **What do I think of the people in charge?** Relationships play an enormous role in the success or failure of change projects. If you have in place a highly credentialed and respected change team, its access to and influence over others can be considerable. When the opposite is true, you are in trouble. You must have observed a number of projects in your organization that were staffed by individuals junior in level, inexperienced, sometimes incompetent for

the task at hand. Change teams of this composition may have been quite inspired—among themselves. But they didn't gain access to the stakeholders they needed to sway, and their projects petered out ignominiously. The credentials of the change team are important.

STAKEHOLDERS CHANGE THEIR MINDS

Different stakeholders will perceive the same changes in very different ways—this is obvious. Less obvious is that stakeholders' reactions and beliefs usually evolve during the project. We have seen change leaders surprised to find their staunchest supporters balk when the change process approaches too close for comfort. As a result, it is important periodically to take the pulse of all stakeholders and assure yourself that you really know how they perceive the unfolding course of events.

USE FOCUS GROUPS

Effective use of focus groups is essential to discover stakeholder motivation. You can issue written surveys or deploy trained interviewers to understand the views and motivations of a large, dispersed group, but focus groups are better. Group dynamics always provide additional insights into intra- and intergroup issues. Focus groups are best kept small, from five to eight individuals. Since an effective focus group can be conducted in one or two hours, even allowing for preparation, summary, and follow-up, you can conduct dozens of focus groups in a month. Consistent use of focus groups can generate hundreds of stakeholders who rightly feel that they have provided personal input to the change process. The more stakeholders feel involved in assessing the need for change and in shaping the nature of change, the more prepared they will be to commit to change and contribute to its success. This is buy-in.

GET PERSONAL

People take change personally. To build momentum, identify the 5 to 10 most influential stakeholders and develop specific, personal programs to sell them your ideas. All of us as individuals—even proven team players and elder statesmen who seem to view everything with the impartiality of their years—are highly influenced by personal wins. If you can communicate to the top 10 individual stakeholders the legitimate personal wins resulting for them from the changes you envision, you will do your change program a great service.

All large organizations have a political land-scape (horizontal view) and a pecking order (vertical view). The political landscape is often surprisingly ad hoc. Not identical to the organizational chart, it is shaped as much by individual character—by those one admires, by those one has reason to fear across the organization—as by position and reporting relationship. The pecking order *is* the organi-zation chart, and it greatly influences behav-ior. As a consequence, individual managers participating in group stakeholder discussions are likely to leave unsaid certain views and issues that you want to hear—and you won't hear them at meetings invisibly dominated by those managers' superiors.

Consider employing a technique we call "Adopt a Manager." Here is how it works. If you have a core change team of 10 individu-als, for example, select the 30 most influential stakeholders and divide them such that each team member is now responsible for three. Each will then develop or enhance personal relationships with the three stakeholders. They should meet with "their" stakeholders (at best, one on one) every few weeks, or more fre-quently, to discuss project activities, go over anticipated changes, float ideas, and solicit their views. This venture will provide impor-tant feedback to the team and gauge on a con-tinuous basis the level of support you can expect from those who will most influence the outcome of your work.

People are motivated by the desire to achieve better conditions than they currently enjoy. This is true for the visionary whose dreams led to the change project; it is also true for the non-believ-ers asking, "What's in it for me?" Motivation is sometimes rational and logical, just as often visceral and emotional. Inspiring others to act anew involves understanding and appealing to their motiva-tions. It is the task of the change leader and the change project team to identify and link the needs (and wins) of each stakeholder to the benefits of the project.

FOUR KINDS OF STAKEHOLDERS

No matter how long your list of stakeholders, it can be divided into two broad groups as depicted in the matrix in Figure 3.1. The horizontal axis represents the spectrum of support you currently anticipate from each stakeholder group. The vertical axis plots what you perceive to be the magnitude of the change impacting each stakeholder group. Your success will depend upon under-standing where each group "fits" in this matrix—and working with them accordingly.

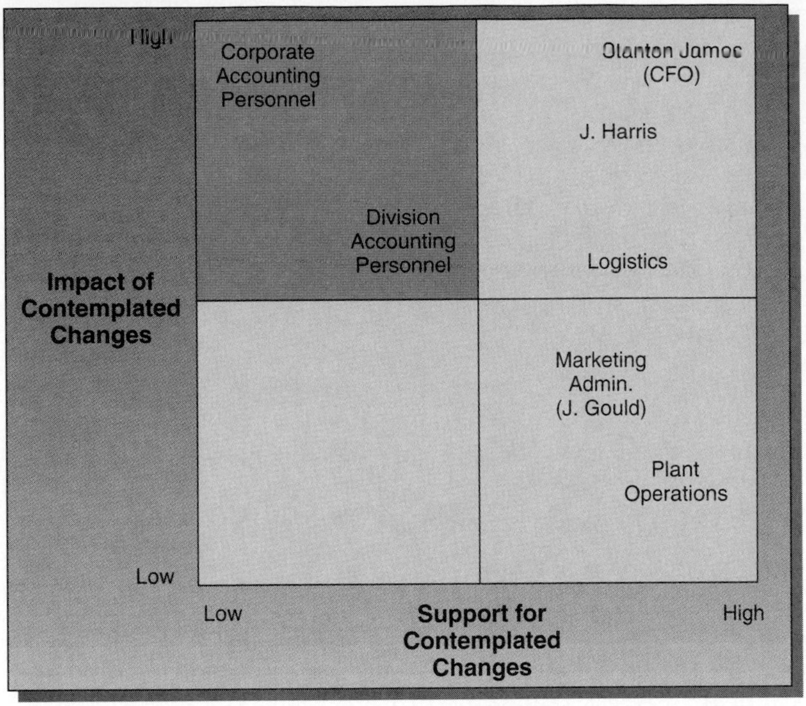

FIGURE 3.1
MAPPING STAKEHOLDER
SUPPORT FOR
CONTEMPLATED CHANGES

The two large groups are:

• **Those supporting change.** Motivated stakeholders are easy to spot. They are constructively rather than unproductively critical, proactive in assuming personal responsibility for the change effort, focused on results rather than excuses; and they treat problems as opportunities. Motivated stakeholders can have a multiplier effect on the change initiative. Their optimism and assurance, communicated to the rest of the organization, will encourage fellow stakeholders to persevere during chaotic or painful periods in the change effort. In assembling a project team, enlisting those who are already enthusiastic about the project will enable you to deploy them as change agents. Such change agents can become the cornerstone of your commitment-building efforts across the organization.

> **Motivated stakeholders can have a multiplier effect on the change initiative. Their optimism and assurance, communicated to the rest of the organization, will encourage fellow stakeholders to persevere during chaotic or painful periods in the change effort.**

• **Those not motivated to change.** Many who are not fired up by your new ideas will sit quietly by. They tend to express their negative perceptions and emotions by skipping project meetings or briefings, offering no new ideas, and refusing to participate in teams. They remain eternally noncommittal. Others can be outright hostile to your efforts. They will work proactively to undermine your project. But it is a serious error to characterize these individuals as criminals. Others can be just as legitimately impassioned about alternative ideas as you are about yours. Work with them. Engage them. Negotiate with them. First and foremost, exercise that high-tech device that so expressly communicates to others that you care about their ideas and want to work for consensus: your ears.

PATIENCE

Stakeholders require a great deal of maintenance. You will spend what seems a disproportionate amount of time eliciting their views and drawing them into consensus, or attempting to do so. But the effort pays. Only in this way can you eliminate sources of doubts and anxiety that otherwise might spread throughout the organization. If you manage to convince some or all of your honorable adversaries concerning the merits of your change effort, you are likely to verify the truism that there is no better evangelist than the convert.

SUMMARIZE STAKEHOLDER POSITIONS

It is a good idea to summarize stakeholder positions and to keep this summary in front of the team. For the purpose, we use the matrix illustrated in Figure 3.2. It will encourage you to summarize stakeholder positions along several important dimensions. For example, the first column summarizes each group's "intellectual"

FIGURE 3.2
CHANGE READINESS
ASSESSMENT (SUMMARY)

Change Requirements / Constituency	Target Group			Customers & Suppliers
	Intellectual Commitment	Emotional Commitment	Required Skills	Required Support
Senior Executives Through Directors	◑	◑	◑	N/A
Plant Management	○	○	○	◑
Plant Employees	◑	◑	◑	◑
◑ Committed and ready / ○ Uncommitted and/or not ready	The belief that change is necessary and the proposed changes are appropriate	The willingness to carry out the planned change and "weather the storm"	The skills required to carry out change and operate effectively in the new environment	The support from others necessary to carry out change and operate effectively in the new environment

CHAPTER THREE

readiness for change—their understanding of the rationale behind the change and their related buy-in. The second column summarizes their emotional advocacy. Emotional buy-in can greatly differ from intellectual support. Those who become resigned to change because they are convinced of its logic may still not have their hearts in it. They can be expected to "go along," dragging their feet all the way. The last column speaks to the support you perceive from suppliers and customers (internal *and* external). Their advocacy or rejection matter to you. With this summary in hand and up to date, you are better positioned to communicate with your stakeholders than if guided by instinct or memory alone. The matrix, however, cannot take the place of detailed plans for securing the commitment to change from each group and/or individual. You may want to consider summarizing individual stakeholder positions as in Figure 3.3.

> **First and foremost, exercise that high-tech device that so expressly communicates to others that you care about their ideas and want to work for consensus: your ears.**

GET ISSUES INTO THE OPEN

Clarifying issues, fears, and opportunities through stakeholder meetings can move some reasonably key players beyond self-concern to the point of imagining and mentally trying out the changes you are sponsoring. Identify these co-workers as potential change agents

Example, Inc. Purchasing and Disbursements Improvement Project				Stakeholder Analysis
Area of Change	**Impact**	**Stakeholder**	**Anticipated Reaction/Issues**	**Comm. Strategy & Planned Response**
Procurement Reengineering 1) Increased Budget Accountability	High	Davis/Jones	• Want more control over spending • May not want to encumber prod. mgrs. • May not want added visibility to their spending • May not want visibility of past failures	Comm. Plan A
		Product Mgrs.	• Most do not want added controls • Do not want added visibility to their activities	Comm. Plan B
		Lippincott/Roemer	• Says historically has never worked • Personally in favor of cost controls • How will this impact his job?	Comm. Plan A
		Breden	• Wants more control over spending • Level of commitment/action unclear	Comm. Plan A
		Mktg. Dept. VPs	• Want more control over spending • May not want to encumber staff • May not want added visibility to their spending • May not want visibility of past failures	Comm. Plan B
		Sharpsim	• Says there are already enough controls	TBD Work into team
		Nelson	• In favor of more cost control/accountability	Work into team
		Steinberg	• Won't want more visibility to spending	

FIGURE 3.3
SAMPLE STAKEHOLDER ANALYSIS

A HARD SOLUTION, A SOFT LANDING

Since its privatization, a European telecommunications company had worked hard to improve its products and services as well as its general reputation. As a privatized entity, the company had to be more responsive than before to market forces, and this was no secret. On the other hand, through its regulatory powers, the government remained something of a shadow boss, often working at cross-purpose to market forces. The company soon found itself between a rock and a hard place. Its hope lay in well-conceived, well-accepted change.

The significant costs associated with offering a high level of service had become a problem for the company because industry regulation forced it to hold down prices, no matter how costly the services demanded by the marketplace. This conflict forced the company to examine how to provide services more efficiently without reducing quality. One obvious solution was to improve the productivity of the work force. Internal studies had shown that much of the engineering staff's time was rou-

tinely lost—for all sorts of reasons. This "leak" offered a perfect opportunity to try to change.

To investigate and make recommendations, the company assembled a project team of people who actually did the jobs and engaged in the processes that needed reengineering. This alone represented an important first: In the company's history, no project team had ever had such an intimate knowledge of its issues, such a clear stake in the outcome of its work. These were the people who would gather information, set standards, and, most important, convince their colleagues that the draft solutions were appropriate and achievable.

The team observed current work methods and analyzed vast quantities of historical data on every aspect of the business. Through this demanding process, the extent of the opportunity for change was closely defined, and this in turn permitted the establishment of benchmarks against which future performance could be measured.

and consider involving them in the visioning process. Getting issues into the open energizes change. And it has a curious side effect that most organizations will welcome: a new level of candor about the company's processes and practices, goals and strategies.

Events moved quickly from that point forward. By persuading key stakeholders—specifically management and union leaders—of the good sense of the change project, the team was empowered to initiate major change. The implementation plan was so soundly constructed that the change team saw it through in what was perceived as a short time frame without disruptions to the business.

The newly envisioned operating model promised to yield significant financial benefits—and began virtually at once to change the attitudes and approach of engineers and of the managers responsible for engineering. The model included a control system designed to quantify on a daily basis the performance of engineers. Line managers were now able to examine the previous 24 hours' performance in terms of service quality and, for the first time, in terms of productivity.

Stakeholder motivation was not left to chance. Targeted communications specific to each group represented a vital step in assuring acceptance and cooperation during this major change. Coaching and training were available throughout the implementation. As each manager came on line, he or she was coached in the usage of the numbers and in actions that would improve performance.

Engineers were not positioned as the "victims" of this new analysis. On the contrary, they were briefed on its measures, and each was offered a week of on-the-job training to step up their activities, where needed, to the productivity criteria built into the control system. Further, the line managers were held co-responsible for productivity gains; no one could sit back and wait for someone else to demonstrate virtue.

The project team was gratified to observe that the company as a whole began to measure not only service quality but also daily productivity. This was evidence of the major success of the change project: It generated not only continually improving measured levels of productivity but also cultural change in the organization. Now widely accepted, productivity numbers are cited in discussions of quality of service results, and the balance between quality and cost is being addressed. Within its own sphere, the project yielded a 20 percent increase in the productivity of *1,400 engineers*—with more to come.

DEVELOP A FORMAL PLAN

As you formulate your changes and envision new business models, a plan to secure the commitment of each stakeholder and stakeholder group should be developed concurrently. It should outline the perceptions and positions of each constituency, including means of involving them in the change process and securing their commitment. It should also define how you intend to leverage the positive attitudes of enthusiastic stakeholders and those who "own" resources supportive of change (e.g., information, access to allies, communications capabilities, policy-making authority, available funding). It should make clear how you plan to minimize risks, including the negative impact of those who will oppose change.

SIMULATE TO STIMULATE

You will get a lot of mileage out of the effective use of prototypes, pilots, simulations, and walk-throughs. Helping your stakeholders visualize change can create excitement about the positive possibilities and generate commitment to change. Be creative in designing means to allow everyone to try the new environment. In Chapter Two we told the story of a change team that carved up cardboard boxes to model new store designs and encouraged employees to try out many alternative configurations and processes. Higher technology is available to help you achieve the same goal. For example, computer simulation tools will help the change team design new processes and answer questions about staffing levels and potential bottlenecks. But the same imagery, projected onto a screen, will help stakeholders visualize the intended changes and excite their interest and buy-in. The goal is to give stakeholders as much advance experience as possible of the new configuration of processes, tools, systems, technologies, and facilities—to make the coming changes as tangible as possible, as soon as possible. Stakeholder input regarding these prototypes is critical to successful change.

> **The goal is to give stakeholders as much advance experience as possible of the new configuration of processes, tools, systems, technologies, and facilities—to make the coming changes as tangible as possible, as soon as possible.**

CLARIFY AND QUESTION UNDERSTANDINGS

Confusion causes inaction, and inaction is virtually sure to diminish stakeholder commitment. Everything that needs to be done, how it should be done, and the structures through which it will be done must be clearly spelled out to stakeholders. Roles and reporting relationships are invariably among the key elements about which you will need to be specific. Since stakeholders will have differing perceptions of many other key elements, you will want to encourage them to ask for clarification whenever they need it, be it from a hot line, a mentor, or the change sponsor. Unfortunately, not all stakeholders will ask questions. Therefore, it is best—best and really necessary—to overcommunicate.

SLAY THOSE SACRED COWS

As we observe organizational change processes, one of our recurrent disappointments is that sacred cows are seldom slain, even in the context of what is billed as wholesale, take-no-prisoners change. In your organization, sacred cows are likely to be grazing freely. While significant change is the objective, and new thinking is the goal, in many organizations *certain* issues just don't come up. In one situation that we observed some time ago, nepotism intervened. For this large family-owned business with a faltering but long tradition of success, real change was imperative. Everybody knew it. But the CEO's sibling was threatened by the implications of change. As a result, much went unsaid and good ideas were discarded. Real change did not occur.

During major change projects, the concerns and objectives of different stakeholders and stakeholder groups often conflict. Conflict can develop owing to the culture of the organization, perceptions of what is happening, conjectures about what is *going to* happen, messages silent or explicit about the role each person will play, relationships among players, the likelihood or remoteness of rewards, and the organizational rites that encourage, filter, or jam opinion. Some of these conflicts will be valid—the issues need to be worked out, and there is no alternative to working them out. Other conflicts will pit sacred cows of the past against organizational capacities and energies that are unquestionably part of the future. What to do about that?

Slay a sacred cow today. Surely long overdue, the act will send a powerful message concerning the seriousness of your change program. And it will marshal support for more change.

A SHORT MEMORY WILL PROBABLY HURT YOU

Change projects have been carried out under many different names and in many forms over the years. Expect some folks in your organization to be fearful, as we said earlier, weary, cynical, even angry when they hear that another concerted change effort is in the wind. When you announce your project, acknowledge the change efforts that have gone before. Consider providing a verbal pocket map of prior change programs. Use your opening communications (see Chapter Four) to link your change effort to previous projects in terms of the skills required to execute them and commonalties of purpose and objectives.

This approach may seem counterintuitive. Many change sponsors want to differentiate their projects and thereby prove their wholly independent worth. But this doesn't fly with jaded stakeholders. They *will* remember those programs, the good and the bad. By honestly showing the fit—or misfit—between the work at hand and change projects of the past and by connecting the dots between the new program and those currently under way in the organization (see Chapter Six), you will signal to your stakeholders that real intelligence and unflinching institutional memory stand behind the new initiative—and their place is on board.

COMMUNICATE CONTINUOUSLY

Newton's Third Law was never so true: An object at rest tends to stay at rest until acted upon by external forces. In change projects, inertia is to be avoided. It is too easy for stakeholders to stay right where they are, especially if they are anxious about the change project or just plain tired. Stakeholders need continuous invitations to become involved, continuous reassurances that they will get their wins. If necessary, build a sense of urgency by dramatizing the results of "business as usual." For many organizations today, that is an ugly picture.

MEASURE READINESS

Measuring stakeholders' readiness for change is a straightforward exercise: interview and survey them. Ask. In one change effort involving a complex shift to new systems, the team felt the need to gauge the readiness of the organization to accept and support what would be a harried, stressful switch. Just before the milestone at

FIGURE 3.4
THE RESISTANCE CHANGE
CURVE

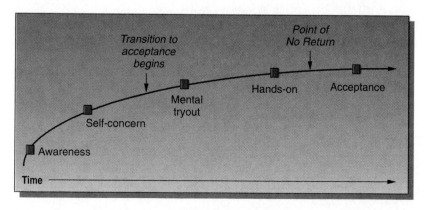

CHAPTER THREE

which the new systems were to go live, stakeholders were requested to fill out a brief survey. Based on six readiness criteria, it asked about their level of comfort with a "go" decision. The answers were scaled from, in effect, "We're dead" to "What are we waiting for?" The summarized results provided an accurate reflection of organizational mood and, since the survey was deliberately not anonymous, the data provided a map for following up with key individuals who had residual issues. This exercise illustrates an effective means of recognizing and addressing motivational concerns before they become obstacles.

> **The active measures, the ones that really count, are not always obvious.**

PERFORMANCE MEASUREMENT AND COMPENSATION

Your existing environment and operating model are firmly rooted in the current performance measurement, evaluation, and compensation systems. Changing what is measured and what behavior is rewarded will promote more rapid change in the way employees do their jobs. In Chapter Nine, we discuss a problem common to most organizations today: too many measures. When there is an overload of measures, only some of them will have real meaning. Be sure to isolate those measures that currently drive behavior. These are the measures you will need to modify or abandon if you expect people to act anew.

The active measures, the ones that really count, are not always obvious. In the course of a reengineering study recently undertaken by a company in the entertainment industry, the change team came to realize that the measures driving the actions of key executives (i.e., highly influential stakeholders) were hidden well within their individual service contracts. Without focusing light on that piece of the performance puzzle, no genuine change could be expected.

PULL STAKEHOLDERS UP THE CHANGE CURVE

As people move through the change process, they experience something like the dynamics of the change curve in Figure 3.4. We interpret the stages as follows:

• **Preawareness.** A sense exists that something needs to be done, but not what, how, or why.

• **Awareness.** Thoughts about what changes are needed, where we want to be, and how to get there are coming into focus but are not yet defined.

- **Self-concern.** The desired environment and possibly some elements of the projects are known in detail, whereupon the concern, "How will this affect me?" becomes primary. At some point between self-concern and mental tryout, the transition to acceptance begins.

- **Mental tryout.** Changes are beginning to be viewed as inevitable, attitudes shift to "How do I make this work for me?"

- **Hands-on.** Simulation of the new environment in the form of pilot projects, prototypes, or training is formalized. The point of no return is reached somewhere between hands-on and acceptance, when the momentum for the change and near-acceptance of change have increased to the point that turning back is unlikely.

- **Acceptance.** The changed order of things is achieved, the new environment becomes the status quo.

As the shape of the curve means to imply, the earliest phases require the greatest effort from everyone. Early in the project, when only a few critical individuals are involved, organizational inertia will make much effort necessary to get the process rolling. Once the effort is under way, momentum and effective commitment building help the process to sustain itself. The real indicator of acceptance is when people change the way work gets done and measurable results are achieved.

Given their early realization that things must change for performance to improve, senior management typically starts up the change curve first. Middle management, often feeling threatened by changes that at least suggest flatter (de- layered) organizational structures, is last up the curve. The primary deterrent to the natural desire of employees for positive change tends to be the fear of job loss. If appropriate, allaying this fear as early as possible frees the most powerful lever of change in the organization.

The metaphor of the change curve is a convenient way to visualize the work of the change team in pulling stakeholder groups through a fairly predictable sequence of attitudes and securing their commitment to change. The team should schedule commitment-building activities in cycles for various stakeholders as they move along the curve. As one group of stakeholders—for example, senior managers—reaches the level of mental tryout on the curve, another group of stakeholders—say, employees—reaches the awareness level. By the time management reaches acceptance and

> **Expect setbacks. Expect roadblocks. Be ready for them, and address them on a case-by-case basis as you and your team encounter them.**

employees reach hands-on, external stakeholders may just be reaching awareness. It goes on and on, until everyone is there.

WHAT TO DO WHEN YOU LOSE TRACTION

No project starts with a strong core of support, builds momentum smoothly—support radiating smoothly across the organization—and concludes with a flawless metamorphosis into the new environment envisioned by those driving change. It just doesn't happen that way in large organizations. Expect setbacks. Expect roadblocks. Be ready for them, and address them on a case-by-case basis as you and your team encounter them.

It is not uncommon for large-scale change projects to stall—to lose traction, we say. This can happen for any number of reasons. For example, you might lose the support of a very influential champion. Your project sponsor may get promoted, transferred, or leave the organization. Any of these things can set you back a step or two. The following are three steps you should consider to regain momentum:

• **Be candid.** If there is conviction on the part of the organization that the kind of change being enacted is necessary, slowing down need not be fatal. If the change was important enough to start, it is important enough to carry on. But don't proceed as if nothing has happened. Don't deny that momentum has been lost. If you elect to cover up the situation, enough people will still feel the loss of momentum and recognize that you are not being truthful. Your candor will buy you support.

• **Inject a customer into the process.** A good way to snap everyone back to reality (i.e., the need to change and change now) is to bring a customer into the process. Customers are candid; they *are* the reality of your organization. Fulfilling their needs is the raison d'être of your organization. Use this reality. Invite several key customers to some focus groups. Let your stakeholders hear their concerns.

Some years ago, a team at Price Waterhouse charged with introducing a new quality management process in our firm thought progress toward our then new strategic imperative—obsession with client service—had begun to lag. The team wanted to reenergize the process. Team members decided to hold a large focus group and invited to it a number of very influential partners and two major clients. The clients were encouraged to speak openly about the services they had received over the last 18 months, and while they were quite satisfied, they also made a few very significant observations that resonated powerfully with those in attendance. For one of the clients, we had just concluded a major project in which the Price Waterhouse team was drawn from offices and practice units nationwide. He told us he was very satisfied with the work, but he had nonetheless felt the weight of our organizational structure within our project team. He was referring to the subtle tug that each consultant's home office or unit must have been exerting during the engagement. That perception had not posed a problem for our client. But, he observed, he could imagine that agenda conflicts, however muted, might be troublesome in another circumstance. This riveted everyone's attention—and gave our change team the renewed impetus it needed.

• **Shake some reality out of your employees.** They know what's really wrong, and they also know more than you'd expect about how to fix it. If you are having trouble swaying middle or executive management, share what the real "value-adders" know about how things are currently done—or not done. Your managers may be surprised out of their complacency or fear and into action. You can use the voice of employees by helping them prepare and deliver presentations to senior management in person or on videotape. If the message is sufficiently unpleasant or unpopular, you may want to protect your people by presenting the facts in aggregate. This still works. Our survey center has helped many organizations find out what their people really think. For one multinational bank, we did a peer survey to inventory management's strengths and weaknesses, to provide a mirror to managers, and to kick-start new lines of communication. Over 300 members of the management team assessed each other in seven areas: technical competence, teamwork, customer skills, leadership, management skills, working characteristics, and overall performance. Each individual received a customized report, and individual and aggregate results were shared with senior management. Results were so useful that this company is planning a repeat performance annually. Hard facts motivate better than almost any petition or admonition.

> **If you are having trouble swaying middle or executive management, share what the real "value-adders" know about how things are currently done—or not done.**

• **Kill something big in public.** If you're really stalled, you may need to do something dramatic—in full view—to get things moving again. Consider persuading a powerful executive to make a really telling gesture. Smash a genuine but undesirable icon. This act will forcefully communicate to everyone that this effort *is* going forward.

Probably the most frequent example of this mode of action is the management shake-up. When things are thoroughly stalled and gloom hangs over the change effort, frustrated CEOs have been known to replace those who cannot or will not change with those who heed the message of change. This strategy can be effective. However, we hasten to point out that there are many powerful icons, other than people, worth nixing. Actions as simple as closing the executive dining room or executive parking spaces can signal important new ways of thinking. In one large chemicals company, the new chairman deserted the corporate dining room and ate lunch with employees in their cafeteria. This alone was enough to herald a new way of operating. Business dropped off quickly in the executive dining room.

BUDGET LOTS OF TIME

Our closing suggestion is to budget lots of time for all the above. It is not uncommon for the project manager to spend the majority of his or her time managing communications to stakeholders and securing their commitment to change. The demands may be irritating at times. We also believe that nothing is more satisfying at the end of a project than to see positive change propelled by others whom you brought into the process.

Large organizations, like large cities, are lasting miracles of management. The volume of products and services delivered at affordable prices to a nation and a world is immensely impressive. But this miracle is not only one of technology, manufacturing, and distribution. It is also a miracle of communication. Your organization includes people now who combine the analytic powers and personal sensitivity to motivate stakeholders in all categories through their clarity, honesty, and exemplary commitment. These are your change leaders. You are probably one of them; this will help you recognize the others.

CHECKLIST   MOTIVATING STAKEHOLDERS

___ Budget plenty of time for stakeholder identification, communication, and motivation. It will save time and effort later.

___ Know thy stakeholders. At the very least, be sure you have identified these stakeholders (as individuals or groups; group stakeholders only where you are sure their stake is the same):

___ Customers   ___ Owners/shareholders/investors
___ Suppliers   ___ Strategic business partners

___ Employees   ___ Management
___ Yourself   ___ Your project team members
___ Community   ___ Regulatory agencies

___ For each stakeholding individual or group, know

    ___ Why the stakeholder is interested in or has a stake in your change effort, and what that stake is.

    ___ What impact your planned changes may have.

    ___ How the stakeholder is likely to react to your planned changes (hint: ask the stakeholder, and listen to the answers).

    ___ The degree of power and influence the stakeholder has over your change.

___ Summarize stakeholders (and their stakes, change impacts, likely reactions, power and influence) simply and graphically on a frequently updated one-page map so that you can read your stakeholder health at a glance.

___ Develop and implement a plan for getting the support and involvement you need, and for minimizing the impact of intransigently negative stakeholders. Your plan must enable you to:

    ___ Clearly communicate coming change actions, their benefits, and desired stakeholder roles during the change process.

    ___ Question stakeholder understanding of the message.

    ___ Get issues out in the open and resolve them.

    ___ Use simulations to stimulate feedback and understanding.

    ___ Notice how and when stakeholder feelings and positions change.

___ When powerful stakeholders don't get excited about your change project's goals but you need their support or resources, determine how you can legitimately tie their personal wins to your project wins. Show how the change is in their best interest. (This works with all stakeholders, but is a key approach for executives, owners, and shareholders.)

___ Remove the roadblocks keeping the best people from serving on project teams. Go talk to their bosses; tell them how their people will come back with new skills, and how they will have contributed to a critical company effort. Offer to provide performance evaluations based on the person's project performance. Then *follow up.*

___ Be sure the project leader is a star who can get things done and whom people admire. You will be able to pick and choose the best team members from among all those who gravitate to this leader.

___ Motivate people in your organization to change by changing how they are recognized, rewarded, and paid. Measure and reward performance that makes a difference.

___ Change people's reporting relationships and how their jobs are structured. Give people a role in making these decisions.

___ Put "resisters" on analysis and design teams. Assessing how work gets done and how bad the problems really are helps convince people that change is necessary. Being part of the solution helps people want to make change happen.

___ Most change projects involve only 1 percent of the employee population to figure out the answer and then tell everyone else. Involve a larger group in figuring out and communicating solutions (rule of thumb: approximately 10 percent of the employee population).

___ When you've hit a stumbling block, acknowledge the loss of momentum (be candid!) and immediately begin rebuilding motivation (see list above: communicating, resolving issues, using simulations, taking stakeholder pulses).

___ If a powerful stakeholder blockade develops, bring the customer into the picture. Nobody outranks the raison d'être of the company. The customer's desires are the ultimate tiebreaker.

___ Another key voice is that of your employees. They know what's really wrong, and more than you think about how to fix it. If management doesn't get it, use survey and analysis results, or—if you really believe in the truth—employee presentations to get the point across.

___ When stakeholder reluctance is holding you back, examine the unspoken messages in your company and send a louder message of the new reality. Sometimes you have to slay a sacred cow or kill something big in public to get stakeholders to take note.

___ And, finally, take heart. For remember what Niccolo Machiavelli tells you of change:

"There is nothing more difficult to carry out, nor more doubtful of success, nor more dangerous to manage, than to initiate a new order of things. For the initiator has the enmity of all who would profit by the preservation of the old system, and merely lukewarm defenders in those who would gain by the new one."

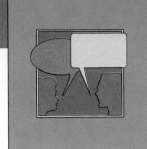

FOUR

Communicating Honestly

onesty is a virtue, but this is not a chapter about virtue. It is about management effectiveness. Where change projects are concerned, the traditional preference of management to restrict and even meter the flow of information to the company at large works against project success. A clear-eyed distinction needs to be made between the kinds of information that truly are management's province and those that need to be broadcast. Old reflexes can skew that judgment. There are almost always penalties for thin, misleading, or sporadic communication in support of major change. There are almost always rich rewards for honest, convincing, well-sustained communication. This is a chapter about building and tending the communications network that supports large-scale change. And it is a chapter about attitudes.

• • •

Not long ago, the receptionist at a walk-in clinic in Virginia was casually browsing the classified section when she came across a help-wanted ad that caught her eye. She felt well qualified for the position; it fit her situation. But upon investigating further, she discovered that it was *her job*. Her employer was soliciting to replace her. Incensed, she marched down to the newspaper and placed an ad in the same column to declare she had quit. She figured, "If I find out via the newspaper, they can find out via the newspaper."

This anecdote illustrates an extreme breakdown in employee–employer communication. But don't think for a minute that this is a one-in-a-million occurrence. In the turbulence that attends broad-based change projects, communication can break down and create extraordinary barriers. On the other hand, communications to stakeholders can be thoughtfully crafted to promote and propel the changes you seek.

Communication is the shadow behind everything you do in the transformation process: It is not the first thing on anyone's mind, but you can't go anywhere without it. Communication is fundamental to creating change, and all of us willingly acknowledge that. Less obvious is *how* to use communications to create the kinds of change you are seeking. No one may notice when your program is working well, but you need people to pay attention, to learn what there is to learn. Worse yet, no one may know when the program is not working well, but in that case you need people to rally to the cause.

Every effective communications program is unique because it is designed and governed by the parameters of the specific project. But all such programs have certain common goals. A good communications program starts by building the case for change. It is tuned to the views and positions of key stakeholders. It is designed to meet their concerns and to provoke them to action. It informs and engages the organization about progress along the road to success, thereby maintaining momentum. It sustains enthusiasm for change by reminding your people of what is at stake as implementation begins. It praises all change leaders and stakeholders when the project becomes a proven success.

HONEST EQUALS EFFECTIVE

In the context of creating and sustaining change, the words *effective* and *honest* are synonyms. Credibility is the foundation of effective communications, and trust is impossible to sustain when the case for change is corrupted by misleading information. Whether justified as politic or as a sheer operating necessity, lack of integrity detracts from the business at hand and can damage relationships among diverse stakeholders who must work in tight partnership during the change process.

The best messages are simple and straightforward. Spend adequate time honing your messages so that they are easy for your audience to grasp and personalize. One of the best examples we have observed of communicating honestly to further a change project involved a chief financial officer who knew the change effort he had in mind would lead to downsizing his staff. He told his staff that the change project was about "creating better jobs for fewer people." The candor is impressive, the message is simple and clear. While it left plenty for some employees to worry about, it had a very positive effect upon the majority. Those who were confident in themselves and in the value they provided the organization saw his message as their hope for a better tomorrow. Your communications program should seek this standard of honesty and simplicity.

There are executives who get into trouble with their organizations despite the best of intentions. This is much less likely when you deliver messages that are true, clear, and not subject to misinterpretation. Even perception matters, as you well know. The appearance of not acting straight with your people will hurt you and hurt the change effort. *You* might survive a crisis of faith; your project might not be so lucky.

> **Even perception matters, as you well know. The appearance of not acting straight with your people will hurt you and hurt the change effort. *You* might survive a crisis of faith; your project might not be so lucky.**

MAKE A PLAN

The shorter your project time frame, the more effective the communication plan must be to achieve the desired outcome. The case on the following page illustrates the benefits of a thoughtful communications strategy and plan.

EXAMINE YOUR INTENT

Sit down and think out what your program should communicate. This is an exercise not just about wordsmithing but about substance. Be sure your message focuses on the logic of the change you have in mind and your communication is couched in terms of business need. Absent clear logic and clear need, your plan will predictably invite skepticism and resistance. Proof of our point is never hard to find. For example, a product company announced internally its intention to switch its fundamental strategy from that of low-cost provider to a focus on getting more new products to market faster than the competition. Unfortunately, the company had not coupled its declaration of strategy with an orderly and well-communicated transition plan. After many false starts, the effort was abandoned. Why? The answer in this case was simple:

CASE STUDY

A Vast Project, Communications Duly Proportioned

One of the world's largest quick-service retail food chains, with billions in domestic and licensee sales, knew it was time to "break the pencil" by adding computer automation support and network communication to each store. The situation was ripe for change. Administrative paperwork had become overwhelming. Outlet managers were spending as much time each week on filling out forms as they were spending on customer service. The answer to this dilemma had to be on the scale of the enterprise: It would be a very large, ambitious answer, or it wouldn't be an answer at all.

And so it was. The chain decided to undertake an $85 million project to put 1,800 personal computers into 1,800 domestic stores in 18 months. The project involved 42 autonomous regions, 38 companies, 8,600 people, and over 300 full-time project field implementation personnel. The requirements were quasi-military in magnitude, and the resulting campaign was probably the largest in the history of American systems development.

As the effort acquired momentum, trained installation and service personnel swept through the country, traveling by day and working by night to install the system. They were restocked by air and land shipments at predetermined pickup points. Their work is a story unto itself—but the other story, no less dramatic, concerns communications.

Project leadership recognized early that clear and flexible communications would be key to the success of this massive project. A communications plan and schedule was created; an 800-number hot line was installed and staffed around the clock, seven days a week; and a full-time person was assigned to handle both internal project and external field and supplier communications. A carefully conceived and stable implementation plan and schedule was reproduced in multiple forms (hard-copy memo, presentation,

Company structures that effectively supported a low-cost provider strategy were not dismantled, while new structures were assembled unpersuasively, in the shadow of the old. Employees heard one strategy but could see the other persisting unchallenged, unchanged. Had the change agents critiqued their communications plan, they might have noticed the flaws of substance underlying it—and done something about them.

reduced pocket card, various electronic media, wall banners, etc.). Over 2,500 copies of the plan were produced and distributed so that all concerned could know at a glance where they were, where they were going, and where to find help if needed.

The leadership group consisted of 14 steering committees, overseen by a control group. Individual and team roles were clearly communicated and reinforced in training sessions. Since many recurrent communications were soon reduced to routine, the highly knowledgeable communications teams could focus on difficulties and unforeseen occurrences.

Every practical communications technology was employed, including voice mail, e-mail, communications network scheduling and document updating, phone lists, and conference calls. All 8,600 participants had ready access to key information and scheduling information. Communication was viewed as everyone's job, and training encouraged the attitude among one and all of never thinking or saying "That's not my job." People at the center of the effort were given all the information they needed to provide answers at once or connect questioners with those elsewhere who had answers.

The project was completed on time, on budget—and judged a grand success. There had been a few problems with suppliers, but overall the project was the largest, most focused collective effort in the company's 40-year history, and a victory.

Lessons were learned. It became evident during the effort that clear and thorough planning, plus dedicated leadership, had resulted in a highly effective communication plan. It also became evident that horizontal communication is just as important as vertical communication, or even more important. The use of every possible channel to enable interchange engendered communications in 360 degrees, bypassing management levels where it would only be delayed or filtered. The team also learned that providing people access to information as needed, on demand, is a very effective communications principle. Finally, it became evident that flexible communication systems allow people to monitor and handle exceptions before they become problems.

ASSESS YOUR POSITION WITH STAKEHOLDERS

Before attempting to move ahead on any communications program, it makes sense to appraise the degree to which stakeholders trust the executive sponsors and change leaders. If credibility is low, the communications strategy must be heavily skewed toward action rather than words. Actions should be carefully selected to support the message you want to deliver and to demonstrate that management is "walking the talk." Employees want to trust management. But actions, not words, flow to the bottom line.

In assessing trust levels, you must determine whether problems are based in reality or on unfounded perceptions. Managers are not always to blame for low credibility. It is not unusual for today's managers to inherit credibility problems from a previous generation of managers. Further, assumptions and suspicions have a weedy energy—they grow everywhere—while trust has to be cultivated.

We were asked to survey stakeholders at an East Coast utility that faced restructuring. Many people with whom we spoke indicated that management could not be trusted. Their perception was based on a false assumption that certain executives knew more than they actually did know. These suspect executives were perceived as withholding information from the rank and file—information they didn't actually have. Trust between the two groups remained fragmented until a dialogue was initiated to make clear who knew what and to help restore the trust needed by management to proceed with the restructuring.

It is worth remembering as a member of the executive management group that your stakeholders will remember (and tend to focus on) the one or two instances where credibility and consistency seemed suspect.

TELL THE TRUTH

Truthful communications can be straightforward, with little potential for misinterpretation. On the other hand, communicating half-truths or messages laden with spin-control will quickly generate a large employee filter of skepticism, through which your words will be scientifically passed; this is likely to deflect or block messages you want people to receive intact. Many organizations begin change projects by announcing to employees there will be no layoffs. When the layoffs occur the remainder of the implementation is severely hampered. Where there is possible bad news (e.g., layoffs) or solidly good news (e.g., no layoffs), tell the truth early and often.

STAY IN TUNE WITH THE CULTURE

The effectiveness of your communications plan is influenced by its consistency with the culture of the organization. In some organizations, effective communication calls for a high degree of professionalism and seriousness, while in others a touch of show business may be necessary to get the attention of stakeholders. When a major toy manufacturer decided to introduce laptop computers to assist its sales force in developing planned orders, highly experienced salespeople understood at once that management intended to alter their conduct of business. To head off the resistance and negativity this was likely to arouse, the company president decided to turn the introduction of laptops into an event by tying it to the annual toy fair, the premier trade show of the industry. The salespeople were enticed into a demo of the system. This deed earned them a button that proclaimed "I saw it!" Those who agreed to try the new tool and create a prototype order were given a button that said "I did it!" In many other environments, this approach might have seemed hokey, but for this particular work force, it was effective.

> **You yourself don't know all the consequences of a change plan, however diligently you try. And yet it is best to draw a line around such truth as is known and clear at any point, and put that out over the airwaves.**

KEEP NO SECRETS

There are very few situations in the course of a significant change initiative in which it is desirable (or even possible) to keep secrets. For the most part, the attempt results in lost trust, diminished commitment, and faltering motivation and cooperation from stakeholders. The rumor mill works overtime in periods of significant change; employees' desire for information becomes insatiable. And rumor mills do not grind out only chaff, they also grind truth and "secrets." It is best for there to be no secrets.

This is hard advice to follow. It goes against instinct. Management information differs from Securities and Exchange Commission-mandated disclosure, membership has its privileges, and so on. Plans evolve slowly, consequences unfold over time— you yourself don't know all the consequences of a change plan, however diligently you try. And yet it is best to draw a line around such truth as is known and clear at any point, and put that out over the airwaves. A video game manufacturer discovered the futility of keeping secrets. While planning layoffs, management threatened probationary action against any member of the planning team who let the secret out. All meetings ended with a shredding session to minimize accidental exposure. When the layoffs were finally announced, management was dismayed to learn that employees had long known about them—people even knew by name and employee number who was going to be given notice! In the end, management lost in three ways: It caused undue stress for the members of the planning team; it lost credibility with the work force who learned the bad news through the grapevine; and any perceived benefits associated with the timing of the information's release were lost.

STRIVE FOR CONSISTENCY

People involved in comprehensive change programs are masters at testing the consistency of messages they receive. The stated vision, mission, strategies, action programs, measures, and other management missives must be consistent to earn credibility with your audience. Inconsistencies lead to confusion and eventually to inaction. Experience shows that people are willing to change—as long as the direction of change is clear and steady. With this in mind, make sure that everyone on the change team acts as a "devil's advocate" in evaluating the consistency of messages. Achieving consistency will also help to prevent the work force from perceiving the change initiative as a flavor-of-the-month.

There is another issue of consistency: Square your change project messages with other company change initiatives. When other change programs are under way, the messages associated with them must be taken into account to ensure the overall weave of messages creates a consistent picture that makes sense (see Chapter Six, "Connecting the Dots").

ACTIONS MUST BE CONSISTENT WITH WORDS

Action is the most persuasive and visible measure of the honesty of change leaders. At one company, executive management talked enthusiastically about the innovative thinking behind its change initiative—but then communicated the opposite by appointing a change team composed of veteran employees who had nothing like earned reputations for innovative thinking. This action sent a very specific message: The "new" organization would not look much different from the existing one. The caliber and level of those chosen to lead a change effort is a key and much-noticed fact. Their selection is an action taken in front of the audience of stakeholders, not a private agreement after which public activity can smoothly begin.

FUEL THE FEEDBACK LOOP

Feedback is critical for you to understand the needs and constraints of your organization and, on that basis, develop workable plans. Feedback also enables you to test stakeholders' reactions to recommended changes. As all successful change leaders know, however, thoughtful feedback needs to be encouraged. Some people are naturally vocal, while others will not easily volunteer information that may nonetheless be important to the change effort. Whether they are shy, afraid of being reprimanded for bucking the party line, or simply undervalue the information they have to share, these people need to be drawn out.

One very effective change leader at a consumer products company had several stakeholders who were reluctant to volunteer information during wholesale changes to the company's distribution practices. At a point early in the change process, he invited several stakeholders to his apartment. After a few beers, he asked his guests to take a yellow Post-It and enter a number indicating their degree of commitment to the change effort—from 1 ("I'm delighted to be part of this") to 10 ("Let me out of here!")—and then place it on their foreheads. He followed up by asking each person to explain. As they answered, the participants provided invaluable information about rumors, concerns, confusion, and other issues that needed to be addressed for the project to move ahead smoothly. The nonthreatening environment and atmosphere of fun helped to fuel the feedback loop. This was not, we think, an exploitative process. It may not suit your specific environment—but something like it can help.

> **You can't beat 'em, so join 'em. Use the grapevine instead of letting your project be abused by it.**

Your listening skills are vital to receiving feedback. If your people do not think you are a good listener, they are unlikely to speak freely and provide the feedback you need. Further, they will rightly expect communication to flow both vertically and horizontally. In this instance, they will expect *you* to provide *them* with feedback. How are you seeing things? What are the problems? What is the view from the poop deck? Absent this breadth of communications, neither your communications program nor the change initiative are likely to be entirely successful. Feedback will serve you well.

USE THE GRAPEVINE

Information pulses through the grapevine as if it were a fiber-optic cable. All companies have grapevines. You can't beat 'em, so join 'em. Use the grapevine instead of letting your project be abused by it. During periods of significant change, there is a corresponding increase in the amount of information passing through the grapevine. Since grapevines are typically lateral and not bottom-up, if you are somewhere toward the top, you'll need other people to be your ears. Surface the rumors concerning what you and the company are doing or thinking about doing. Rebut inaccuracies and quash untruths—but without haste. Communicating truthfully, early, and often to your stakeholders will be of significant benefit.

Stakeholder cooperation at a US airline was shaken when the grapevine reported that the sponsoring executive had a salary of $2 million. The executive heard the rumor, assembled his staff, and announced that his actual salary was $600,000. Even though most of the people in the room and all the people "out there" on the grapevine made much less money, he established instant credibility and succeeded in maintaining it through the remainder of the change initiative.

> **Verbal communication is useful for setting expectations regarding the desired results of change, the approach to be followed in getting there, and the differing roles of people in the change process. Unfortunately, this is not enough.**

A major East Coast financial institution has learned how to make good use of the grapevine. The company has implemented a rumor mill bulletin board within its e-mail system. Anyone with access to the system can enter what he or she believes to be a "legitimate" rumor, one that might concern or confuse employees. A few key executives then have a short time to respond to the rumor by clarifying what is fact and what is not. This is a wonderful tool: It converts rumor quickly into fact where warranted and stalls misinformation before it is amplified by the law of rumor propagation into a major issue. By automating the grapevine, this company is able both to exercise reasonable control over the spread of misleading information and to convert the grapevine into a valuable communications tool.

One can speculate, of course, that corporate appropriation of the grapevine opens an ecological niche for a new species of grapevine to root and flourish. Therefore, return to the top of this section.

BE AWARE OF NONVERBAL CUES

Studies have shown that as little as 7 percent of communication is verbal. This doesn't mean that verbal (or written) communication is useless in change projects—verbal communication remains the best way of orienting people inside and outside the organization to the need for and nature of change. Verbal communication is useful for setting expectations regarding the desired results of change, the approach to be followed in getting there, and the differing roles of people in the change process.

Unfortunately, this is not enough. Too many change leaders do not recognize the potency of body language as they address their stakeholders. Tone of voice, physical gesture, and image often send a much clearer message than words alone. All of these must be consistent with spoken or written words. The stakeholders in your audience will watch for nonverbal cues in order to gauge the sincerity of your spoken and written words. Few of us have a professional actor's awareness of our nonverbal messages, but there is a dependable way to send the right messages: telling the truth. Truth tends to coordinate what we think, how we feel about issues at hand, and how we move and sound as we examine those issues with others. This coordination does not depend on personal type. A bold, aggressive leader telling the truth sends the right nonverbal cues, but so does a more analytic, soft-spoken leader.

LISTENING IS COMMUNICATING

Listening is generally regarded as a passive activity in which the listener is acted upon by the communicator. In reality, listening is also a powerful communications tool, essential to the well-being of your project. How well you listen (or whether you listen at all) tells your audience much about your mind set: Do you make clear that you understand points and later demonstrate that you have listened by bringing those points into what you say? Do you interrupt

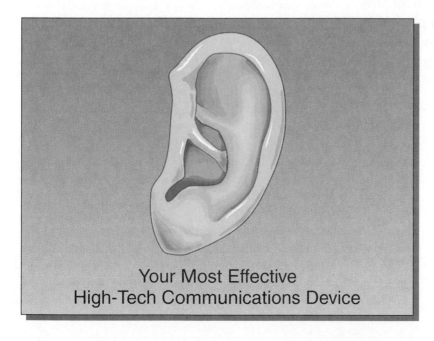

Your Most Effective
High-Tech Communications Device

FIGURE 4.1
YOUR MOST EFFECTIVE
HIGH-TECH
COMMUNICATIONS DEVICE

speakers to give your own opinion on the subject, and show your disapproval of their points of view? As the leader of a change team, your ability to listen sends the message that the voice of the organization is being heard and that its needs will be reflected in the change vision.

A company hired a team of consultants to develop process and organizational recommendations to improve profitability. Rather than positioning itself visibly in the midst of things, the team chose to set up in a work area separated from those who might be affected by their recommendations. This superficially logical action—why should temporary folks occupy prime real estate?— sent a perhaps unintended but powerful message: We are the experts, and the wishes of the organization will play a negligible role in our recommendations. This doomed the team's recommendations before they were announced. The stakeholders within the organization did not "own" the team's recommendations and, in the end, none was successfully implemented.

Compare this to the situation at another company trying to implement a series of significant changes in finance and human resources. Here the consulting team threw itself into the arena with the lions and tigers. Its members were visible, and they listened. People who would bear the brunt of change were involved and able to air their opinions. The team sought out and freely discussed issues with the organization's stakeholders. The stakeholders were again consulted as recommendations were finalized, and their review comments and suggestions were incorporated. Because stakeholders played a role in creating their own futures, they returned the compliment by supporting the revised processes and systems and working to make them succeed.

Because stakeholders played a role in creating their own futures, they returned the compliment by supporting the revised processes and systems and working to make them succeed.

As an effective change leader, you are listening to stakeholders. But it also important to assess how well they are listening *to you*. At the outset of a change project, when you first begin to

build systematically your case for change (see Chapter Two), you may discover that many of your staff are predisposed to doubt or fear large-scale change. They may not really listen, although they will give every appearance of listening. Be prepared for this situation; counter it with honest, useful information delivered consistently and, if necessary, repeatedly.

ASSIGN COMMUNICATIONS RESPONSIBILITIES

In any significant change project, communication is a full-time responsibility and a line job, not a staff job. It should not go to someone in the public relations department who is working on 12 other projects. It demands the creation, and attention, of a communications czar who is close to the action. This individual will design and lead communications programs that carry the change team's message but also help the team understand stakeholder needs and collect stakeholder feedback. Your czar will almost certainly not carry out every detail alone but *will* ensure that messages are properly thought out and delivered at the right time to the right people.

The communications czar should be part of the change leadership in order to remain fully informed of the change process as it unfolds.

LEVERAGE YOUR MESSAGE WITH TECHNOLOGY

Numerous technologies can be used by an executive team to communicate its case for change to the organization. "Groupware," for example, will allow you to establish an electronic town hall where employees can access information, air rumors anonymously, and so on. And as noted in an earlier section of this chapter, groupware or e-mail systems give change leaders the opportunity to respond without delay to questions or rumors with facts.

Price Waterhouse was the earliest large-scale user of Lotus Notes, a powerful groupware system, which now connects 15,000

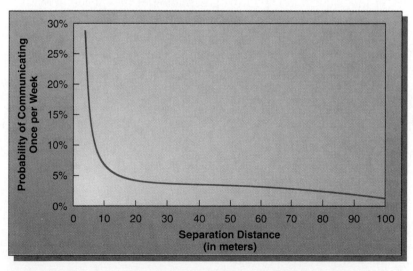

FIGURE 4.2
WHY IS THE CHANGE TEAM LOCATION IMPORTANT?

Studies have shown that communication is much more likely to occur between team members if they are located close together.

Source: Allen, *Managing the Flow of Technology* (Cambridge, MA: MIT Press), p. 239.

FIGURE 4.3
DEVELOPING A
COMPREHENSIVE
COMMUNICATIONS PLAN
In managing change, it is difficult
to communicate too openly.

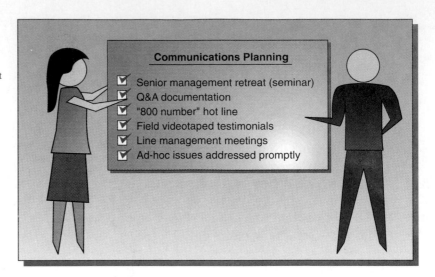

Price Waterhouse personnel around the world and provides access to a stunning variety of informational databases. A central value in our culture—sharing knowledge—has acquired in Lotus Notes a technology platform that remains for us something of a miracle, although we have been using the system for some years. This paragraph is an ad for Lotus Notes only insofar as the system exemplifies an egalitarian approach to information. Change initiatives thrive in an atmosphere that offers people as much information as they want and need.

Other useful technologies include voice mail and closed-circuit television, as well as the array of technologies mentioned in our case study of a massive systems installation in a nationwide fast-food chain. These technologies have been relied upon by many large corporations to speed access to accurate information and to defeat misinformation.

THE FIVE CS OF SUCCESSFUL COMMUNICATIONS PLANS

As you design and implement your communications plan, key attributes should be kept in mind. The plan at best will be:

• **Candid**. Always tell the truth; your employees will probably know when you don't.

• **Contextual**. Provide your stakeholders with the "big picture" as you explain the relevance of the project to the company.

• **Constructive**. Guard against counterproductive comments that work against team and stakeholder unity.

• **Consistent**. Ensure that verbal, written, and nonverbal forms of communication are consistent from message to message, and that your actions support your messages.

• **Continuous**. Provide ongoing reinforcement of your commitment to the change initiative.

Further, a good communications plan will identify:

- Who the stakeholders are.
- Communications objectives for each.
- Communications actions for each.
- Messages to be sent.
- Tone of messages.
- Media to be used.
- Who will serve as spokesperson(s).
- Expected outcomes.
- Optimal frequency of messages.

Clarifying these issues will help you focus on the unlike concerns of specific stakeholders and also give you a clearer vision of where stakeholders have common concerns. Such common concerns are sometimes so obvious they are overlooked—witness the case study on the following page.

The successful outcome of the high-tech company's change effort was due in part to the fact that its key employees all spoke a common language. This is not always so, however, as we illustrate by the case study on pages 86–87.

How'm I Doing?

The best way to determine whether your communications program is working is to ask a cross section of stakeholders for their perceptions of the project and their understanding of its most important features. If their answers agree to some reasonable degree with the thinking of the executives driving change, messages are getting through. Another important indicator of communications effectiveness is the absence of significant surprises among those affected by the change effort. Surprises indicate that expectations have not been properly communicated or that information has not reached people in a timely manner. Use survey documents and focus groups at frequent intervals to test the effectiveness of your communications program.

> **Guard against counterproductive comments that work against team and stakeholder unity.**

REBUILDING COMMUNICATION TO REBUILD THE BUSINESS

A $300 million high-tech manufacturer of process control equipment faced shrinking market share. Within memory, the company had enjoyed a 50 percent share of its key market and a reputation for innovative products, quality, and customer service. However, by the date at which this case begins, the company had lost 15 percent of its market share, competitors were all over the landscape, its products were outdated, and its stock price had begun to register the bad news.

Acknowledging that its previously successful formula no longer worked, management decided to assemble a team to characterize the problem unmercifully, identify root causes, and take action. In this context, a project was initiated to eliminate a major problem: a slow, inefficient order fulfillment process.

The team's analysis of the delivery cycle uncovered communication breakdowns at nearly every step of the process, from field sales through manufacturing and installation. Further investigation revealed that the most serious communication problems pre- vailed between Engineering and Manufacturing, and they were of a very interesting kind: Engineering was releasing products and changes faster than Manufacturing could keep up. Products were "thrown over the wall" as they passed from one department to another with inadequate documentation, training, and support. As a result, Manufacturing and the field sales force fell farther and farther behind. Errors, financial loss, confusion, and finger-pointing were the rules of the day. Communication between the departments could not have been worse.

Since the problem was both miserable and promising—there was no failure of innovation here, only a failure in process management—the reengineering team felt in its bones that a straightforward solution could be found. The team went to work and found that it could accomplish a great deal by tackling the communication component of the problem.

- A management presentation about the problem was written and distributed.

FOCUS THE MESSAGE FOR STAKEHOLDERS

Grand ideas and intentions are likely to be grand flops if they are not well communicated to the work force. Your initial communication represents your best chance (in some instances, your only chance) to bring to your side the diverse stakeholders in the organization. In Chapter Three, we discussed segmenting your stakeholders into groups. Here are the essential insights into communicating with these groups that we have gleaned from previous assignments.

- Management developed common goals for the two departments and agreed on new information systems to support these goals.

- Project team members were mobilized into a communications network, each knowing to whom information must be passed in real time.

- Specific communications vehicles (e.g., status reports, key memos, product information, joint meetings, etc.) were created and shared among the departments and those working with the departments.

- Engineering staff were added to Manufacturing teams, and vice versa—a magnificent strategy so obvious that one could easily fail to see it.

- Brown bag lunches were organized in both department work areas to keep the communications channels wide open.

The result of this many-sided change effort focused on communication was immensely positive. Manufacturing is now an integral part of Engineering's product development process. When product developers finish documentation and training materials, they remain assigned to products well into the manufacturing and installation life cycle. As we write, the product-to-market cycle now is 15 percent faster (the goal is 50 percent), and orders are filled 20 percent faster (the goal is 36 percent). Market share is rising, products are becoming more advanced, and profitability is up.

And people are talking with each other. One of the most interesting benefits of the effort is improved interaction among people at all levels in the two departments. Management spends more time on the floor; informal social functions are more numerous. The spirit that was present when the company was smaller is starting to return. In every dimension, this case study exemplifies honesty in communication, leading to honest effort and a very sound result.

- **Top management.** This may or may not be the first group of stakeholders to recognize the need for change, but until they do, it is a safe bet that a reengineering effort will not succeed. Their full support and commitment are critically necessary. On occasion, even when the president or CEO recognizes the need for change, he or she will encounter resistance from the top management team when trying to sell the idea. About which, see the next paragraph.

- **Executives.** If they do resist, this typically means their plates are already full—or that they are single-mindedly focused on items

CASE STUDY

IF YOU AREN'T CLEAR THE FIRST TIME . . .

As a large consumer goods company discovered, "once over lightly" does not characterize effective communication where change projects are concerned. Undertaking a major reengineering project in the company's manufacturing division, the MIS department gave a somewhat cursory overview of things to come to top management and key division players. The presentation was honest but far from thorough enough to convey that the people in the room were being asked to sign up for the mother of all reengineering projects. They assumed the project was a large but basically traditional systems project that would require minimal executive attention once it got under way.

When the reengineering team's process analysis began homing in on business strategy, critical success factors, and performance measures, the executives finally realized the project was bigger than they had bargained for. The reactions began—along these lines:

- "What do you mean we can't manage the business by looking at cost-per-case alone?"
- "We can't touch that; it's a union issue."
- "We don't need reengineering. We're already world-class."

- "We're different; we just can't operate with lower inventory."

To some, it was time to circle the wagons around their sacred cows. To others, the true scope and nature of the project came as a pleasant surprise. MIS tried to keep the project on track, but the dearth of firm support in word and deed from top operations executives encouraged rumors of its imminent demise. Resources became hard to get; executive steering committee meetings were inexplicably postponed. The project entered the crossroads. Either operations management would endorse the first principle of reengineering— "There are no sacred cows"—or the project and its anticipated benefits would have to be abandoned.

The only forum where the divergent views of MIS and operations could be resolved was the executive suite. A meeting was called with the CEO to discuss the issues and to ascertain whether he wanted serious reengineering or just a systems implementation. As he listened to the opening salvos between adversaries, the CEO gathered that his ongoing, deliberately visible support for enhanced systems to further the company's long-term business

that will ensure year-end bonuses. Unless they are brought to understand the real drivers of change and the negative consequences of a failure to change, they will withhold their support. Be alert to "lip-service only" responses. Review the need for

CHAPTER FOUR

strategy was not understood by one and all as support for reengineering. To some people in the room, systems meant hardware and software; to others, systems enhancement meant reworking the organization in its primary dimensions—process, organization, people, and technology.

When, as the saying goes, all eyes turned to the CEO, he made a statement that would later resonate throughout the company's communications network. He made it crystal-clear that his definition of reengineering was broad. It meant not just systems work but also change in depth, change in breadth, sparing no sacred cows. Reengineering meant methodical pursuit of big results.

Within days, the company newspaper ran a lead article detailing the CEO's unambiguous support for the project. A training program on the methods and purposes of reengineering was quickly constructed and made mandatory for all employees. On his side, the CEO assigned a widely respected operations vice president to be wholly responsible for the project. Further, all company executives were invited to a meeting at which the CEO communicated his message about the importance of the project's broad scope and stretch goals.

After this project relaunch, which included not only a clear mandate but also improved accountability, the reengineering continued on to a very successful conclusion. Sacred cows were gored; performances measures were revised; dramatic organizational changes were made; and the system is now being implemented successfully.

It is evident from this tale that even high-level executives do not necessarily know what you mean when you refer to reengineering—until you spell it out for them. It is also evident that the MIS department could have done its groundwork better by explicitly and publicly connecting its efforts to the CEO's support. If the folks at the top of the house aren't *heard* cheering, it doesn't matter much that they *are* cheering. Training also comes up in the case study—in this instance, too late. Training for those who will be affected by the change project should start early. Finally, it is worth noting that the MIS sponsors of this project knew how to begin again. They weren't afraid to halt the train when they discovered the executives weren't on board. They understood that they would never get to their destination without them.

new performance measures and incentives (see Chapter Nine, "Measuring Performance").

• **Middle management.** This group is often criticized as least receptive to change, and in many client companies we have found

FIGURE 4.4
FOCUS THE MESSAGE FOR
STAKEHOLDERS

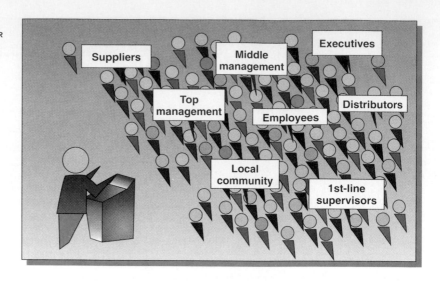

this to be true. However, keep in mind that midlevel managers take their cues from the top. If a senior executive's communications with his or her direct reports lack consistency, honesty, sincerity, and timeliness, and if those communications are not creatively reinforced over time, the natural tendency of this group of stake-holders is to consider the message a passing fancy that everyone will recover from in time. This response is all the more likely when the senior executive is notorious for jumping from one program to the next. There are many issues to examine here, including the possibility that the senior executive would benefit from a refresher course in communications. But the gist of the matter is clear: A strong and persuasive series of communications from the top will unquestionably sway the middle ranks.

• **First-line supervisors.** This group of stakeholders, more than any other, fears lack of control over their careers, their direct reports, and their environment. Intuitively they may understand the case for change, but they may not yet be trained or empowered to assist in the implementation. When this is so, stress levels rise and survival instincts take over. Unless they understand what is happening around them and expected of them, they can resist contributing their wholehearted involvement in the process.

• **Employees.** This is the largest constituency within your company, and without their support and desire for the success of the change initiative, the project is doomed. Union companies will find this especially true. Why? If you think back over your own company's labor history, the evidence is probably right there. In most cases, the work force wanted a union because of lack of trust in management. If this premise is true for your company, and if

CHAPTER FOUR

management-labor relations are characteristically tense or periodically pass through periods of tension, the task of creating a credible case for change will be much more difficult. Under conditions of tension, trust can be gained by sharing information honestly, communicating frequently, and directly addressing employee concerns on a routine basis. As trust grows, cooperation will begin to fill the void previously occupied by indifference or acrimony.

If employees—union and nonunion—do not understand your intent, they will jump to negative conclusions and try to protect themselves from what they take to be a threat. Canvass this stakeholder group frequently for their issues and concerns; ensure that your messages demonstrate consistency and honesty and respond to their issues and concerns.

• **Stockholders, investors, suppliers, and distributors.** Unless they understand how the changes you desire will positively affect their investment or business relationship, these stakeholders can convert their perception of instability into the real thing. You do not want them nervous; you do want them to see and agree. Everything we have layered into this chapter about honest, accurate, and thorough communications tuned to differing stakeholder perspectives should help you gain the support of these critically important stakeholders.

We wrote at the beginning that this would be a chapter not about the virtue of honesty but about the effectiveness of honesty. Truth draws people together, gives them a clear sense of where they fit, and invites them to contribute their best. Half-truths and such have no equivalent power. However, the truth about change projects is often complex. As a consequence, it is not enough to have the shiny ideal of honest communication. One has to do one's homework, and do it over and over as the project unfolds, so that what one communicates is not just well-meaning but meaningful. Business has a higher intellectual content than many imagine.

CHECKLIST   COMMUNICATING HONESTLY

___ Set a standard of honesty and simplicity for all communications: honest enough to be both startling and reassuring, and simple enough to explain to your child or your grandmother.

___ Use your existing communications infrastructure where it meets standards for honesty and simplicity.

___ Make communications in your change project someone's express responsibility. Create a communications czar if you must to be sure that communications are effective.

___ Have, use, and continuously refine a communications plan. It should include:

    ___ A clear statement of the project's change goals and how communications are intended to help achieve those goals.

    ___ An accurate and frequently updated stakeholder analysis, since stakeholders are your audience(s).

    ___ Up-to-date audience information needs analysis.

    ___ Assessment of appropriate communicators, communications styles, and media.

    ___ A schedule of minimum, proactive communications based on the need to build commitment; prepare teams; gather information or feedback; monitor or report progress; surface or resolve issues.

    ___ A means to use the grapevine: surface rumors, squelch inaccuracies, and plant truths.

___ Build time into the schedule for show-and-tell with interested stakeholders, to display work in progress and tell how the project is going. Set up weekly events: brown bag discussion lunches, visits to work sites, cross-functional gatherings.

___ Be careful to select communication techniques and media that are appropriate for the message. Some options you may not have thought of:

    ___ Phone mail with daily updates.

    ___ Messages in paycheck envelopes.

    ___ Electronic mail or groupware.

    ___ Computer-based training.

    ___ Videos (music videos, too, not just the standard talking-head variety).

    ___ Personal correspondence (thank you notes, brief letters to team members at home).

    ___ Rumor hot line or bulletin board (answer within 24 hours of the posting of a rumor or question).

    ___ War room with charts, posters, and other graphics illustrating work in progress and progress made.

    ___ Off-site workshops or seminars (however, don't think travel is a treat for someone who's already on a plane week-in and week-out).

___ Invite executive management to speak with the project team as a whole, in subteams, and in one-on-one conversations. Everybody wins: Project teams get a morale boost; executives get a close look at what's happening; and the project becomes viewed as a mission-critical endeavor.

___ Use face-to-face communication as much as possible. Coach middle managers and team members on the right answers to the inevitable questions ("Am I going to lose my job?").

___ When the news is bad, tell the truth early using simple honest language in a fairly normal tone or style. Don't be overly light or heavy, and don't try to hide bad news with euphemisms.

___ Be sure the project team does most of the communicating; carefully select those messages that really need to come from executive management.

___ Unions represent special challenges. If you are inexperienced in dealing with unions, get advice early and often from shop stewards and labor lawyers to enhance your ability to be open and honest and to build trust.

___ Establish a representative system whereby large or dispersed stakeholder groups (not already represented on the team) designate someone to participate in the project and report back to the group on project progress and happenings. The reporter can also act as the project's eye and ears, relaying problems the stakeholder group may be having.

___ Hone messages until they are immediately graspable and perceived as relevant by each stakeholder or stakeholder group.

___ Be sure that all communications:

    ___ Tell the truth.

    ___ Are delivered by credible communicators.

    ___ Are in tune with your culture.

    ___ Are consistent with other messages, actions, and company initiatives.

    ___ Ask for, enable, and use feedback.

___ Follow up. Meet deadlines and commitments. When your communications promise or offer something, be sure to deliver. If something happens and you can't, explain immediately and make things right. Any indication that you are not playing it straight with your stakeholders will hurt you and the change effort.

___ Don't stop. Messages must be repeated at least three times to sink in. When you do cease a certain message or use of a certain media or spokesperson, announce the cessation and the reason for it. That keeps people from getting nervous about what's going on behind the scenes.

FIVE

Empowering People (Really!)

*Employee empowerment is probably the least under-
stood, most anxiety-provoking term in the lexicon of change management. Senior executives often perceive it as the politically cor-
rect way of alluding to two horrible prospects: organizational
chaos and personal abdication of power. Empowerment need mean
neither of these things. Empowered employees make more decisions
and have more accountability, but in expansive, successful organizations there are more decisions to make. Each has his and her own
sphere of responsibility. It can work. As to loss of personal power:
in growing organizations with empowered employees, executives
learn to move flexibly from one group to another to solve problems,
examine opportunities, and provide encouragement or rude awak-
enings as required. It is a happier thing by far to work this way.*

• • •

The earthquake that rocked the Los Angeles area in 1994 will be
remembered for as many reasons as there are Southern
Californians. Surprisingly, for employees in many organizations
who were called upon to respond to the chaos and devastation,
memories of the earthquake's aftermath are not necessarily all bad.
Immediately after the quake, these people had to make decisions

and make them quickly. They had to do what was best for customers and the companies they worked for. They had to use their own judgment and do things to the best of their ability under remarkably difficult circumstances. In short, Mother Nature had done what most of their organizations had yet to do: It empowered them. They, in turn, demonstrated just how effective they could be.

Organizations should not need an earthquake to discover that empowerment can make their work force more productive without sacrificing essential leadership and controls. But many fail to recognize the importance of empowerment as a source of positive change until they are forced to "try something, anything" by the needs of their businesses and obviously unhappy customers. The reason for this reluctance is not hard to find. Most businesspeople would agree that empowerment is a buzzword. It has the suspicious aroma of a consultants' flavor of the month, a door opener that lets those rascals in. It even seems a bit New Age, as if the next step past empowerment is pyramid power. There are as many off-putting "war stories" about empowerment programs as there are success stories. Also, the thing has so many names—employee involvement, morale improvement efforts, gaining commitment, culture change, employee satisfaction. By whatever name, the bottom line for most organizations is that empowerment does not work well, although it could and should.

FIGURE 5.1
THE TRUTH ABOUT
EMPOWERMENT

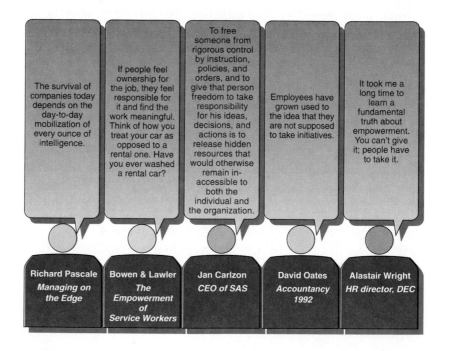

The survival of companies today depends on the day-to-day mobilization of every ounce of intelligence.	If people feel ownership for the job, they feel responsible for it and find the work meaningful. Think of how you treat your car as opposed to a rental one. Have you ever washed a rental car?	To free someone from rigorous control by instruction, policies, and orders, and to give that person freedom to take responsibility for his ideas, decisions, and actions is to release hidden resources that would otherwise remain inaccessible to both the individual and the organization.	Employees have grown used to the idea that they are not supposed to take initiatives.	It took me a long time to learn a fundamental truth about empowerment. You can't give it; people have to take it.
Richard Pascale *Managing on the Edge*	Bowen & Lawler *The Empowerment of Service Workers*	Jan Carlzon *CEO of SAS*	David Oates *Accountancy 1992*	Alastair Wright *HR director, DEC*

WHAT IS IT?

Many managers seem to think about empowerment in much the same spirit as the Supreme Court justice who said of pornography, "I might not be able to define it, but I know it when I see it." Figure 5.1 illustrates the views of a small sample of businesspeople and academics—and we find truth in all of them. However, the definition we believe to be most helpful is the following:

> **Empowerment is the creation of an environment in which employees at all levels feel that they have real influence over standards of quality, service, and business effectiveness within their areas of responsibility.**

Empowerment is the creation of an environment in which employees at all levels feel that they have real influence over standards of quality, service, and business effectiveness within their areas of responsibility.

MISCONCEPTIONS

It will be helpful to look at what empowerment is *not*. There are two common misconceptions—first, that most employees lack power. But think about your own staff. Do they have the power to impact quality? To satisfy or irritate customers? To work together enthusiastically and cost-effectively—or not? They have all of these powers and more. The issue is not that employees lack power; the issue is that their power is often not effectively channeled toward meeting organizational goals.

The second misconception is that empowerment means giving power away—that empowerment programs represent a sort of voluntary coup d'état that diminishes the breadth of responsibility of upper management. This misconception often prevents management from properly communicating empowerment, even if some type of empowerment program is under trial. The truth differs from these misconceptions. Empowerment does not entail giving up anything, least of all senior management's role in leading the organization toward success. By empowering people you are not abdicating power but sharing it with others who also have a say in the organization's future. You are also acting on an expansive concept of your company's future: Empowerment does not divide a pie of unchanging size in some new way; it promotes production of additional pies that feed everyone at your table more richly. With proper empowerment, you *increase* the power of the organization. And if you do not empower your people in ways that make sense, there is a reasonable chance that someday nothing much will be left to have power over!

The Case for Empowerment

The case for empowerment is stark. We live in a world in which products, technologies, and even strategies are quickly copied. This is no reason to walk away from the game, but it does mean the playing field is constantly leveled anew by you or by your competitors. Under these conditions, good products, a tight cost structure, efficient distribution mechanisms, dedication to customer service, and first-class information are sheer necessities. And these things will falter somewhere along the line unless your company has the ability to build, release, and focus the energies and talents of your people. The most reliable, least replicable competitive advantage in today's business world is a work force, from the executive suite to the customer service representative, that cares passionately about the company's success, which is its own.

> **The most reliable, least replicable competitive advantage in today's business world is a work force, from the executive suite to the customer service representative, that cares passionately about the company's success, which is its own.**

This is where the concept of empowerment enters. In an empowered environment you can:

- **Decrease costs**—because fewer people are required to direct, check, supervise, monitor, coordinate, and so on.
- **Improve quality and service**—because high performance is built in at the source. The vast majority of people *want* to do a good job. Let them!
- **Act quickly**—because smart people on the spot see more quickly how to solve problems and capitalize on opportunities. Free people from bureaucracy and engage their minds and you will resolve problems with impressive speed. Throw away the notion that senior executives understand the customer or the product better than frontline staff.

Communicating Is Not Empowering

If some degree of empowerment is in everyone's best interest, why isn't it working and what can organizations do to make it work? More than a few obstacles stand in the way. The biggest is the most curable: Many executives still fundamentally misunderstand what it entails and how to present it to their managers and employees.

Communicating is not empowering, but many executives confuse the two. Let's say that in years past, senior management directed the company's affairs in traditionally close-to-the-vest style and provided a palliative trickle of information to employees at large through the company newsletter. Now, in the name of empowerment, management repents its former sins and holds huge employee meetings to provide an overview of strategy, processes, and results and to encourage people to care. This is good, but not necessarily good enough. While there can be no empowerment without communication, there can be communication without empowerment.

One of our clients, a large UK-based manufacturer, convenes annually a series of road shows. All employees are exposed to the organization's performance, prospects, and strategies. This is a very good practice. But the company doesn't stop there. It actively builds empowerment through:

- Appraisals of managers *by subordinates.*
- "Open book" luncheon discussions at which junior staff have the opportunity to quiz senior managers.
- A cash budget for each and every employee, to be spent on any personal development activity the individual chooses, from learning Japanese to music lessons. Wasted treasure? You would want to look at the company's results and employee turnover rate before reaching a hasty conclusion!

ACTIONS ARE WHAT MATTERS

Sometimes senior executives declare that their goal is empowerment, but their actions contradict them. When push comes to shove, they revert to making all key decisions. We are in difficult terrain here because some matters do need to be kept confidential—for example, negotiation toward a major acquisition. However, if you wish to create an environment of trust, respect, and openness, you had better mean it and follow through in all respects that serve the best interests of the business. The penalty for mixed signals can be harsh: a terrific drop in employee morale, which is bad for business.

Experience shows that most employee groups want to improve their organizations. They can be receptive to empowerment initiatives—provided the substance of the initiatives makes sense to them. We recently conducted a survey in a major clearing bank to assess the progress of an empowerment program. The results illustrate the potential in such programs for misunderstanding, miscommunication, and anxiety. The empowerment program focused on shifting responsibility further down the hierarchy from the head office to the branch staff who actually deal with customers. As perceived by the bank's staff, the four highest barriers to making empowerment work in their particular context were the following:

1. Managers and staff have heavy workloads and little time in the working day. This concern was centered on whether managers would have sufficient time to coach staff in their new roles and whether the staff would have time for training and learning. This is almost always a serious issue. Moreover, it is one that must be dealt with. If the organization is too busy to improve, nothing will change. After an initial effort, the gains from empowerment will result in a lighter, not heavier, workload.

2. At this stage, staff can see the benefits more clearly than do branch, regional, and head office management. Management is often slower than staff to grasp the benefits of empower-ment. After all, what's in it for them—other than less power and control? As we have said earlier in this chapter, the resolution to this problem lies in helping managers see empowerment as a shift in their role not a reduction in it. Management can now spend much more time working on strategic direction and people development and less time on the minutiae of implementation.

3. Although middle-level managers are not yet clear about their roles in empowerment, they do see that it may mean very different working practices—and they see that they may end up the losers, even the job-losers.

4. Other concerns center mainly around cash advances, although local teams have no express wish to change current arrangements. This is the "give them an inch and they will take a mile" misconception. Managers often worry about empowered teams going AWOL and changing everything in sight. The bank managers expressed great concern about the dangers of changing the cash advances process. However, the teams had never even suggested a change in this process. The managers' general anxiety was being channeled into a very concrete, but irrelevant, concern. This illustrates the need for specificity; general talk about empowerment is bound to raise concerns. It is only when you can identify specific changes that their benefits can be evaluated objectively.

None of these misunderstandings are uncommon. Make sure that your own efforts avoid these pitfalls.

EMPOWERED TO DO WHAT?

When organizations launch empowerment initiatives, they often unwittingly choose to involve employees in unsuitable activities. Either employees are asked to focus on activities so mundane as to be insulting (conclusion: the organization doesn't care about them) or they are asked to focus on matters so clearly beyond their skills or experience that they become frustrated. Empowerment works best when the focus is on implementing pieces of the company strategy or addressing issues that employees greatly care about—for example, quality and productivity.

> **Managers often worry about empowered teams going AWOL and changing everything in sight.**

A client in the aerospace industry has formed eight "action teams." Team members rotate from team to team, but the mission of all eight is identical: to search for major improvements in eight core processes; to boldly go where no one has gone before; to think out of the box, around the box, above the box—whatever it takes to generate *better change.*

How Much Is Enough?

Empowerment is not a cure-all. No one sensible would argue "the more, the better" in all instances. Some organizations can benefit from a high level of empowerment, others need not go so far. The significant potential costs associated with empowerment should not be ignored:

• **Greater investment in recruitment.** It is critical to have the right people. Not everyone is comfortable in an empowered environment.

• **Higher training costs.** Empowerment doesn't always come naturally. Often a significant investment in developing teamwork, problem-solving, and facilitation skills is required.

• **Higher wage costs.** Empowered people tend to know their worth, to be critical to your success—and to command higher compensation!

• **Potential for inconsistent service delivery.** When you share authority with people, they will almost certainly not use that authority in identical ways. You have to manage carefully so that your employees' unleashed desire to serve customers doesn't end up costing you the shop.

Given that empowerment has potential costs, how do you decide how far to take it? To this purpose, we divide empowerment into four categories along a continuum. The model starts with a condition of simple awareness in which very little change in job activity actually occurs, and it progresses by stages to a high level of empowerment and job change. Managers can find the appropriate level of empowerment for their organizations by clarifying five issues, all of which should influence their policy:

FIGURE 5.2
CATEGORIES OF
EMPOWERMENT

Awareness	Dialogue	Participation	Empowerment
Performance data provided	Time taken for regular 2-way discussions	Extensive team working	Structured by accountabilities
Centrally defined tasks	Changes occur, albeit gradually	Decisions taken at appropriate levels	Manager as coach
Management through procedures	Management-determined pace and direction using individual's input	Manager acts as leader and facilitator	Real-time responsiveness
Top-down control		Initiative is encouraged	High levels of personal responsibility
Task/procedures-focused training	Comments and views are requested	Management by objectives, not directives supported by appropriate style	Focus is external to customers and drives excellence
	Customer-handling focused training	Personal management and interpersonal skill training allowed	Problem-solving and project-management skills are fundamental
			Profit sharing and employee ownership

Increasing degree of involvement

- What is our business strategy?
- How loyal are our customers?
- How complex are our activities?
- How predictable is our environment?
- What types of people do we employ?

While none of these factors alone dictates what is best for your organization, taken together they can lead to the right answer. Whichever mode you adopt, this much is certain: Things will change. Consider Figure 5.4. How accurately does it model the average staff person in your organization? How great a shift will empowerment entail? Is your goal achievable?

ALTERNATIVE LEADERSHIP STYLES

The change in behavior of the empowered individual is significant. However, an even greater change is required in the behavior of the enablers—the managers who do the empowering. The four-stage model helps us here again. Each stage from awareness to empowerment implies a different style of leadership behavior.

In the awareness mode, the leader's role is the traditional one. He or she plans the work, allocates the resources, and directs the effort. Little decision making is shared with staff, but interpersonal relations are not necessarily distant or strained. Giving direction does not inevitably generate a dictatorial style.

In the dialogue mode, the leader adopts, in effect, the role of a salesperson. He or she plans the work but gains cooperation through discussion and effective coordination of resources.

The participation mode takes discussion a stage further by actually involving workers in problem solving. The leader's role is to facilitate the cooperative problem-solving process. He or she relinquishes some positional power but remains first among peers to help the group achieve success.

The empowerment mode is the real thing. The leader concentrates on building the environment in which the team can best do its job. He or she coaches and monitors but makes every effort to avoid participating directly in decision making for which the team has authority. A consequence of this style of managerial behavior is that the leader can undertake this role concurrently with several teams. An interesting issue is raised when the team fails in some objective—as all teams do at some time. In the empowerment mode, the occasion is truly regarded as a learning opportunity. The team leader is held accountable for the mistake, but great effort is put into identifying and rectifying the root cause of the failure.

The change in behavior of the empowered individual is significant. However, an even greater change is required in the behavior of the enablers—the managers who do the empowering.

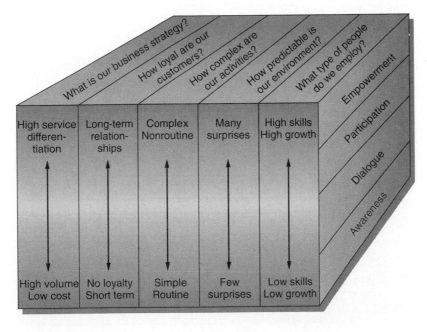

FIGURE 5.3
LEVELS OF
EMPOWERMENT

MORE MISCONCEPTIONS

As we asked earlier, if empowerment is so important, why isn't it more common? Four common misconceptions concerning its implementation stand in the way:

• **Misconception 1:** "No sooner said than done." Managers have no trouble accepting that the effort required to build new facilities, develop enhanced information systems, or launch a new product line will be measured in years, millions, and blood, sweat, and tears. Yet when it comes to achieving competitive advantage through leveraging human resources, there seems to be a belief that it can be achieved overnight for peanuts.

> **There is no silver bullet. To create an empowered environment requires changing many of the things you do. Empowerment is not a program so much as a pervasive style of leadership.**

• **Misconception 2:** "TQM—or JIT or HRM—is the answer." No off-the-shelf item from the ideas warehouse will solve all problems. TQM or JIT, and the empowerments they imply, may be very important for your company, but not in isolation. There is no silver bullet. To create an empowered environment requires changing many of the things you do. Empowerment is not a program so much as a pervasive style of leadership.

• **Misconception 3:** "Just buy a solution." Consultants can take you only so far. They can educate you about the degrees of empowerment, provide a blueprint for empowerment that fits your

FIGURE 5.4
EMPOWERMENT
CHARACTERISTICS

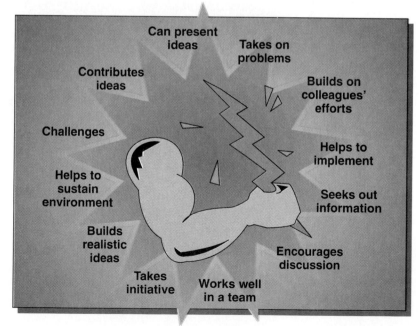

CHAPTER FIVE

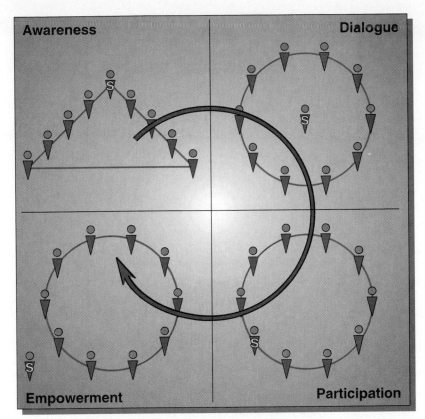

FIGURE 5.5
LEADERSHIP IN THE FOUR
LEVELS OF
EMPOWERMENT

Awareness

Dialogue

Empowerment

Participation

Source: Adapted from John O. Burdett, "What is Empowerment, Anyway?" *Journal of European Industrial Training*, Vol. 15, no. 6 (1991).

needs, assess your people's readiness, and help you implement. But they are the catalyst, not the stuff of the experiment.

 • **Misconception 4:** "Just tell them, loudly, to take the initiative." Coercive empowerment programs don't work. You can't order someone to feel powerful. Your approach to achieving empowerment needs to foreshadow the goal, in the sense that you demonstrate your willingness to work cooperatively with employees to redefine roles. You will need to let everyone in on the game.

These are the misconceptions to avoid. Skirting them, moving forward, you will need to focus on five imperatives (see Figure 5.6).

1. BUILD THE CASE FOR CHANGE

Creating an empowered environment is a more humane way to manage. But if this is the only perceived benefit, empowerment will never last. You need to build the case on business grounds. The question is, "How will empowerment lead to more profit?"

FIGURE 5.6
FIVE IMPERATIVES OF
EMPOWERMENT

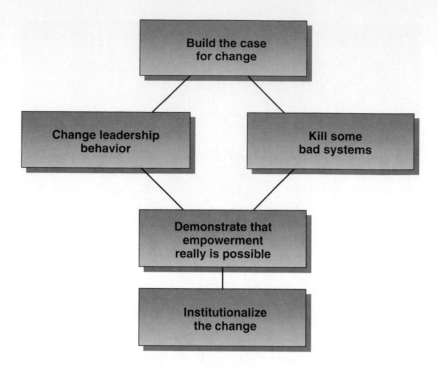

Figure 5.7 illustrates the thinking of the clearing bank mentioned earlier in this chapter. Its senior executives brainstormed and listed all the empowerment opportunities they could uncover and then attempted to quantify their commercial impact. This analysis was enormously influential in persuading the skeptics to give empowerment its chance.

SOUND OUT YOUR PEOPLE

Empowerment opportunities are one thing; feasibility is another. It does not automatically follow from the existence of large potential benefits that an organization is ready to implement against every opportunity. How receptive is the work force to change? Employee attitudes and expectations have been extensively researched in recent years to support change programs. One survey of employee attitudes, titled "Postcards from Employees," gathered information and insight from approximately 50,000 employees in various organizations, industries, and geographic regions, and at many levels of those organizations. The goal was to clarify how a better understanding of the "audience" for change can promote more effective change processes. Striking a responsive note regarding empowerment and involvement among employees at all levels, the study uncovered what employees wished to convey to their supervisors and their perceptions of their own organizations.

Three major points from the postcards are:

• **"Nothing here is ever fully implemented."** Be it a reengineering effort, TQM, a customer service improvement program, or any number of other initiatives, employees were cynical as to whether anything really improves or changes. Their organizations are nonetheless committed, at least on paper, to employee empowerment. To what end are people empowered if they don't believe their efforts will generate results?

• **"I want to be customer-driven."** Although the majority of employees said they love working with customers and derive satisfaction from helping them, many believed that their organizations create barriers to serving customers. They want a clear path from the customer's needs to resources that meet those needs. Consequently, they expressed the belief that empowered employees should be able to change the processes, systems, and other functions that further—or hinder—great customer service. However, many reported they cannot. To what end are people empowered if policy and procedure prevent them from making the positive changes in their own zones of the organization that they know to be necessary and feasible?

> **Although the majority of employees said they love working with customers and derive satisfaction from helping them, many believed that their organizations create barriers to serving customers.**

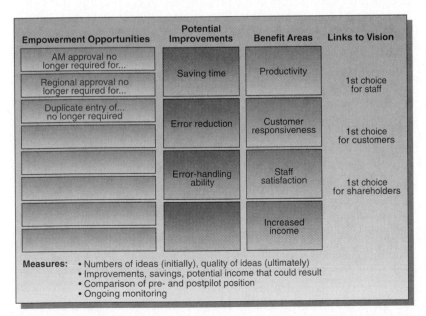

FIGURE 5.7
EVALUATING
EMPOWERMENT
OPPORTUNITIES

• **"Don't yank me around."** Above all, employees want to know the truth and crave consistency. They do not want to hear one day that employees are empowered only to see something soon after that delivers the opposite message.

Our research, and the work of many other research groups, indicates that most organizations have staff who will respond well to increased empowerment. They are waiting for it.

2. CHANGE LEADERSHIP BEHAVIOR

This is critical. Whatever you do to change the systems, structures, and processes of the organization will come to nothing if you do not change the behavior of leaders. Your executives—particularly your senior executives—have to walk the talk. Since many executives have grown up and succeeded in decidedly unempowered environments, expecting a quick shift is unrealistic. You may need to provide training, coaching, and other learning opportunities to help your leaders grasp in what ways they can benefit the organization and themselves through behavioral change. This imperative may seem irritating to senior executives with long histories of successful, hands-on management. This is a classic opportunity to "build the case for change" with sensitivity both to where people are coming from and where the company must go if it is to succeed in years to come.

> **People are unlikely to believe that you are serious about empowerment if they still have to fill in two requisition forms for a box of stationery. Send out a hit squad.**

Moses toured the Sinai peninsula for 40 years with a generation that was not ready for the challenges of the Promised Land. This is not a good corporate model, and we would hope that your organization will not need to adopt it.

3. KILL ONEROUS SYSTEMS

People are unlikely to believe that you are serious about empowerment if they still have to fill in two requisition forms for a box of stationery. Send out a hit squad. A company we admire sent off a cross-functional, multilevel project team to hunt down all archaic practices. This was Project Stop. Its results were amazing. The team found dozens of people fully occupied with compiling statistics nobody read. It found authorization practices requiring multiple signatures that were nothing but rubber-stamp time wasters—if A signed, B signed automatically.

Blow all this away. Show that you are serious about change.

4. DEMONSTRATE THAT EMPOWERMENT IS POSSIBLE

Put some teams to work on real business issues, but be careful to hit the right level. Don't start with issues so strategic that no team outside of the executive suite could possibly score a win. On the other hand, avoid involving people in trivia; they won't thank you for empowering them to choose the color of filing cabinets! By selecting real business issues that fall squarely in the domains of the individuals, teams, and networks to which you assign them, you will be well on your way to empowering people in ways they can value. When they come up with innovative solutions, reward their success. This will encourage others to join the effort when it is their turn.

5. INSTITUTIONALIZE THE EMPOWERED ORGANIZATION

Genuinely empowered organizations typically have three distinct structural features:

• **Few management layers, wide spans of control.** It is difficult to feel empowered with eight levels of management above you. De-layer; get rid of the bureaucracy. Jack Welch's efforts at General Electric set the example. Welch, the chairman of General Electric, has made great strides in creating the "boundaryless company." He has cut management layers, reduced the control of the head office, and empowered local management. All with great effect.

• **A small, facilitative head office.** Sharing power down the hierarchy should affect not only nonmanagerial staff but also managers. They too need to be empowered. A large, cumbersome, and directive head office is unlikely to create an environment in which managers feel free to share power and take risks. Percy Barnevik of ABB seems to have hit the nail on the head. ABB has consistently emphasized that the role of the head office is primarily facilitative. All profit responsibility is shifted down to the managers of largely autonomous business units.

• **A process-based structure.** Strongly functional structures discourage cross-border problem solving. The management silos tend to be so deep that it's difficult for people to reach across to work together. By aligning your structure with the organization's core business processes, you can go a long way toward breaking down functional barriers and freeing people to work collaboratively. A good example here is Rover, the UK automobile manufacturer, with its emphasis on creating a "learning organization." Rover has successfully transformed itself from a company with serious

UTILITIES DO IT

Few sectors are perceived to be more averse to change than the utilities industry. After all, large organizations with entitled work forces have not traditionally been ideal candidates for sweeping organizational change.

One major West Coast utility tried to be different. Although the company was successful by any standard, senior management was not satisfied. Anticipating market conditions and planning for a more closely monitored regulatory environment, management reached the view that the company's ability to change and employee willingness to buy into change had to improve dramatically. A group of six vice presidents was assigned to *make it happen*, although *it* initially remained undefined.

The task was clearly important, despite its open-ended quality, and everyone anticipated another reorganization. To employees this meant very little would change; their lives would get neither better nor worse. Well, one thing would change: the titles and office locations of vice presidents. As one supervisor said, " Same old horses, same old glue." But this initiative would be different. The key was employee involvement.

There was no magic at the beginning of what would later be recognized as the most successful change project ever in the utilities industry. As in many other such projects, a group of vice presidents went off-site to think about things. In addition, a consulting firm was selected on the basis of a track record of working well both with senior management and with employees at all levels. Perhaps it is here that a bit of magic began: The utility was not interested in a black box solution that would have little effect on employees.

The vice presidents gradually articulated their goal. The structure, processes, and culture of the existing organization were driven by the traditional regulatory mentality. This

industrial relations problems to one that many regard as a model of teamwork and collaboration. They have invested significantly in the skills of their management and staff.

Experience shows that close attention to each of these five issues, from building the case to institutionalizing change, will enhance your chances of success. But you would be right to ask what time frames are required to work through the entire process.

was no longer adequate. The organization of the future had to be driven by external customers and internal clients. With this goal in mind, the project team decided to involve employees heavily in the creation of a new structure that would, in turn, empower them. The vice presidents and their consultants created a vision of the new organization: flatter, less complex, attuned to the needs of the client/customer.

When the design was completed, they shifted to communicating with and monitoring the rest of the organization. Nine steering teams made up of employees representing various parts of the company were given responsibility for implementation. Each team was assigned a functional role such as engineering, human resources, or supply and transportation. Each team was responsible for building on the structure already developed and for satisfying the resource requirements to ensure success.

Although there was a consultant on each team, the tasks, outcomes, and authority rested on the shoulders of team members. Involvement snowballed. Each member of each of the nine teams became captain of a subteam of employees whose working lives would be affected by the design for change. At the height of the effort, approximately 5,000 employees were involved. These employees knew they were materially influencing the decision-making process, and they were convinced that a better organization would emerge.

The success of this effort to involve large numbers of employees in reshaping the organization was measurable. As implementation went forward, costs were reduced by 10 percent, and an organization designed to serve the client/customer prevailed. Just as important, a new model was established in which employees could accurately view themselves as agents of change, not its victims. At a time when many organizations are struggling to define and implement empowerment programs that make sense, the utility's success makes clear that if employee involvement is handled correctly, little can prevent change initiatives from being implemented. The employees will do it.

Figure 5.8 illustrates the thinking of one of our clients, an automobile manufacturer, on the issue of timing. Of course, every situation is different, but a two-year timeline is often reasonable.

A FINAL REMINDER

There are costs, but the benefits can be huge. It is not easy, but it can be done. The critical success factors are:

FIGURE 5.8
EMPOWERMENT TIMELINE
AND MILESTONES

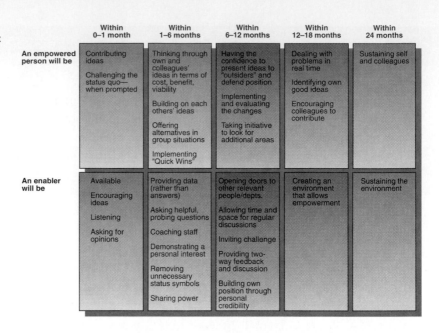

	Within 0–1 month	Within 1–6 months	Within 6–12 months	Within 12–18 months	Within 24 months
An empowered person will be	Contributing ideas Challenging the status quo—when prompted	Thinking through own and colleagues' ideas in terms of cost, benefit, viability Building on each others' ideas Offering alternatives in group situations Implementing "Quick Wins"	Having the confidence to present ideas to "outsiders" and defend position Implementing and evaluating the changes Taking initiative to look for additional areas	Dealing with problems in real time Identifying own good ideas Encouraging colleagues to contribute	Sustaining self and colleagues
An enabler will be	Available Encouraging ideas Listening Asking for opinions	Providing data (rather than answers) Asking helpful, probing questions Coaching staff Demonstrating a personal interest Removing unnecessary status symbols Sharing power	Opening doors to other relevant people/depts. Allowing time and space for regular discussions Inviting challenge Providing two-way feedback and discussion Building own position through personal credibility	Creating an environment that allows empowerment	Sustaining the environment

- Long-term commitment. Target some quick encouraging wins, but think of empowerment as a new way of managing.
- Well-managed staff expectations. Transformation will not be achieved overnight; there will be pain as well as gain.
- Senior executives must walk the talk. At some point your key people have to demonstrate that change begins at home.

People in business organizations are always sorting each other out. This person is terrific—reliable, innovative, a problem solver. That person is none of the above—turn his desk to the wall! This sifting is natural in any alert organization, and it tends to help. In empowered organizations, sifting goes on with relentless speed. There are fewer hiding places, more responsibility, more accountability. Leaders unexpectedly emerge; cultivate them. And people who talked a good game will let you down. The organization becomes more transparent. This is a good thing. It will help you develop leadership at every level. The business you share with all these people will benefit.

___ Build the business case for empowering people. Determine and quantify the benefits you expect to achieve through empowering your people. Then think through whether the degree of empowerment you want can be implemented in your organization. What enablers (information systems? management training? changes in performance measures and compensation?) will be required, and what will be the cost of that implementation?

___ In choosing to empower, make sure all of management understands it will be a fairly long process involving investments of time, money, and possibly other resources. Commit to this investment before announcing empowerment.

___ When announcing empowerment, manage staff expectations. This is not a program that ends. Nor does empowerment happen overnight. Your first empowering act should be to encourage staff to push themselves and management in the right direction (yes, most employees know what the right direction is).

___ Change leadership behavior. Provide training, coaching, and other learning opportunities to help your managers learn to walk the talk.

___ Get rid of as many authorization procedures as possible. This may require predefining decision and spending rights with a great deal more autonomy.

___ Turn people loose to solve real business issues. Authorize them to change things. Give them the information they need. Reward their success.

___ Create an organization that looks like a change project team, so that people don't have to keep forming and reforming teams: few management layers, wide spans of control, small but facilitative head office, process-based structure.

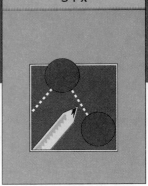

SIX

Connecting the Dots

One management discipline is in short supply in many companies. We call it connecting the dots. It involves a mandate to analyze the coherence of ongoing change programs and the courage to include some in—and include others out. "Including in" does not necessarily mean merging programs, although it can mean that. It often means firming up and warming lines of communication so that related projects enrich each other and have no further reason to compete for resources. "Including out" is rarely a punitive venture, nor need it result in damaged careers for valued managers and employees who worked hard at what they thought was the center. Senior executives who connect the dots, and project champions who help them do so, are the winners in the serious and consequential game of large-scale organizational change.

• • •

As a child you probably had a puzzle book filled with small mysteries—"What's wrong with this picture?" puzzles, and almost certainly some connect-the-dots puzzles. There before you lay an indiscernible pattern of numbered dots. Taking your pencil, you connected the dots and the image revealed itself. Magic.

The unrelated pattern of management programs and performance improvement initiatives that surely exists within your organization today presents this kind of puzzle to your employees. New management tools surface every year or two. Their goal is to improve business performance in an increasingly competitive world. Each has unique levers, emphasis, analysis, and rhetoric for *increased* cost-effectiveness, profitability, and sales; *better* organizational effectiveness and utilization of assets; *higher* quality and employee loyalty. When we connected the dots as children, we had to go at the task patiently until the picture took shape. The same holds true for the array of programs in your organization. Only by connecting them will you see which "dots" belong to the picture you envision and which fall outside that picture. By communicating to your employees how the dots connect and to what purposes, you will help them grasp the picture—and see their places in it.

Most organizations reaching for high performance have launched a number of these initiatives over the past few years. The odds are excellent that several are under way in your company at this very moment. They are almost certainly not all of equal quality and potential impact. The enthusiasm and energy behind some is likely to be waning. Others are probably building momentum and force like a wave approaching the coastline. Unfortunately, when some of those waves hit the beach, they will flatten and recede, leaving a few dazed crabs behind. Such outcomes are not your goal, nor the goal of this book.

THE FLAVOR OF THE MONTH

Like the latest diet that promises "a new you," there is a downside to multiple attempts at change. Inside the organization, they can easily become the flavor of the month or—as one of our clients puts it—management by magazine article. In the worst circumstances, they generate internecine warfare as the champions of each flavor try to differentiate and justify their projects. As programs come and go, those that fail to have truly noticeable and positive impact can damage your corporate culture by encouraging resistance to change among employees.

The reality of the modern multinational organization is that many *do* have multiple programs springing up across the organization. The best-managed multinationals carefully balance individual and group initiatives with the need to work together toward common objectives. The many formal improvement efforts bubbling through your organization probably result from the initiative of managers who are intent on improving their operations. A company that fails to place initiative among its guiding values and to celebrate its men and women of initiative seldom achieves preeminence.

INDIVIDUAL EFFORTS AND THE GREATER WHOLE

But balance you must, sort you must. When your employees are involved in or aware of three, four, or more seemingly unrelated improvement programs—like so many dots in a child's connect-the-dots puzzle—you cannot assume they will perceive an impressive unified picture. They see individual stars but miss the constellation. Unfortunately, the same is often true of a company's senior executives.

Companies need to work hard to connect the dots. As an executive involved in change programs, you will want to build and communicate a consistent, integrated rationale in support of programs under way. Or drop them. No one can seriously expect employees to put in their best-ever efforts on a special project (overtime, weekends, etc.), when they can barely see the leverage and business results expected from *their* project in combination with other projects. Nor can you expect maximum benefit to the enterprise from synergy between programs. In fact, expect conflict as program and project sponsors vie for the best resources. These are two good reasons for connecting some dots—and dropping others as gently as possible out of the picture: synergistic business results and fired-up workers who know what they're about.

THE SCIENCE OF CHANGE AND THE ART OF SLOGANS

Change programs seem to beget slogans. One of the most mysterious we've come across is: "To travel hopefully is better than to arrive." Unfortunately, if you fail to connect the dots for your employees, you may never arrive. A slogan like this one conveys a confused sense of purpose—a willingness to be easily swayed by whatever is perceived as *the next generation* of improvement techniques, rather than focusing on the unachieved possibilities in projects already undertaken. More important still, it betrays a lack of organizational direction. Where is this company going? What does it need to be? The slogan gives a troubling sense that no one on board really knows.

As programs come and go, those that fail to have truly noticeable and positive impact can damage your corporate culture by encouraging resistance to change among employees.

The science of change in large organizations is evolving rapidly, and it's an exciting field. But it is neither progressive nor exciting if employees feel a greater passion for their dynamic program than the end results it is meant to achieve. Without an integrated picture, characterized by realistically demanding performance measures and stretch goals, you will almost certainly be thinking—in a year or two—that the new science of change in large organizations was a flavor of the month.

It is largely up to you as a corporate leader to apply the new thinking and methods so wisely that the results ultimately speak for themselves.

HOW MANY DOTS ARE TOO MANY?

Your organization is large and complex enough to spawn—and to need—multiple concurrent change programs. But how many? Attendees at a Harvard Business School (HBS) conference on "Managing Business Transformation" listed the following as those things most driving them and their organizations to change:

- Pressure to cut costs.
- Pressure to hold down prices.
- More competitors, often on a global basis.
- Opportunities to benefit from new information technology.
- Changes in product/process technology.

The same group reported an average of *five* concurrent change projects in their organizations. What did they list as programs most likely to be under way simultaneously? Customer service and continuous improvement topped the list. Others included:

Total quality management.	Establishing a learning organization.
Reengineering/business process redesign.	Focus on core competence.
Autonomous or self-directed work teams.	Downsizing/right sizing.
	Pay for performance.
Establishing a network organization.	Time-based competition.
	Strategic alliances.

Those sampled considered two to three of their average of five programs to be "extremely important" or "very important." Further, they believed the very existence of multiple efforts to be problematic for their organizations. They had discovered that *simultaneous* and *coordinated* are definitely not synonyms. Some organizations bring to mind that Cold War catchphrase, "peaceful coexistence": turf war is ready to break out at the merest perceived slight.

What is life like in an organization with multiple improvement projects? Middle managers in a position to add value to several different projects are apt to feel increasingly vulnerable to what they perceive as conflicting demands. Daily life becomes like a game of tug-of-war—and these valued people are the rope. Because each project is championed by a different executive anxious for his or her own project to succeed, the situation for those who can ably staff the projects may be exceedingly difficult. As they are bombarded with requests for time to support or to serve directly on various teams, where does their allegiance belong? Your organization cannot excel if assignments are made primarily on the basis of muscle and first-come, first-served, rather than on the basis of an integrated picture that centrally displays the company's highest goals.

> **An ill-organized swarm of "high-priority" programs drains resources and diffuses the energy that makes change happen.**

CONCURRENT PROJECTS, CONCURRENT CONFUSION

Your organization cannot stand still. You need to innovate. You need to empower managers to improve their results. And no single, all-encompassing change or performance improvement project will satisfy every real need. As a consequence, multiple programs will surely figure in the corporate landscape for some time to come— like various religions, each with its disciples, zealots, and critics.

Yet it is clear that *too many* concurrent programs can conflict with and undercut your organization's real work—supplying and serving customers. An ill-organized swarm of "high-priority" programs drains resources and diffuses the energy that makes change happen. When the attendees at the HBS conference were asked how well their organizations integrate multiple programs, fewer than one-third reported the programs were well coordinated with one another. The remaining respondents said their change programs were separate, and a number admitted their programs were conflicting, confusing, and poorly understood by employees.

Surprising? Not really—because the management discipline that we call connecting the dots, although very important to successful change programs, has not yet been widely mastered or recognized. Further, each manager understandably operates within his or her own sphere of influence. It is tough enough for most managers to drive positive change "at home," let alone abroad in the organization. But this leaves a management gap. Few (too few, we think) address the organization as a whole.

Someone at the top must connect the dots.

A Tale of Inefficiency

When the dots aren't connected, forget efficiency. A large US-based consumer products manufacturer recently had as many as six major performance improvement programs simultaneously under way. High-initiative executives in marketing, finance, operations, procurement, and sales were the project leaders. Each carried a banner inscribed with a key message such as TQM, reengineering, cost reduction, or activity costing. The effort put forward by the various executives to coordinate these programs (and their sizable investments) was for the most part ad hoc. Where it was formal, it was mostly bureaucratic. In reality, the programs operated in virtual isolation from one another. From time to time representatives from other departments or initiatives would be invited to project steering committee meetings. But the issues of governance and decision rights were fuzzy at best.

The results? As you may imagine, the project sponsors uniformly concluded their projects had "gone well." Gains were achieved. But in our view an enormous opportunity was missed because no one insisted on coordinating some of the efforts more tightly and on merging others that belonged together. In several instances, approaches to organization and technology conflicted and, after the fact, had to be reconciled. The lack of coordination led, in our view, to substantial duplication of effort and waste.

A Matter of Leadership

Coordinating concurrent change projects is a leadership challenge. The pattern of coordination—and its attendant, often difficult decisions—must be thought through and set in motion by someone with enough authority to influence the organization from top to bottom. When conflict and confusion threaten, a senior executive of real weight is needed to sort things out. Such a person can pull initiatives together—connect the dots—by downplaying differences and focusing on the commonality of change project goals. He or she must be able to see how the dots fit together, how the finished picture will further the mission of the enterprise as a whole.

More specifically, this highly placed change agent must be ready and willing to prioritize goals, rationalize activity, and *make tough choices*. He or she must work to ensure that the best resources are directed into the most important projects for the sake of the organization as a whole. He or she must be able to influence the key (read: most powerful) stakeholders. Finally, the change agent must be capable of forcefully directing the actions of others while remembering that in the long run, employee empowerment is the engine of successful implementation. What we mean by empowerment is revisited in the next section and fully discussed in Chapter Five. In this section we discuss its specific use in connecting the dots.

With these qualifications in mind, it should not be surprising that this responsibility often goes right to the top. However, the "top" need not be corporate headquarters. If change projects have proliferated at the operating unit level, the task of connecting the dots—and deciding which dots genuinely belong to the emerging picture—may justly fall to the chief operating officer.

LEADERSHIP THROUGH EMPOWERMENT

The senior executive responsible for connecting the dots must realistically recognize that one person alone cannot drive change. He or she will almost certainly need to empower project and program leaders to help out. Empowerment means not just having the authority to do the job but also the appropriate knowledge and tools to do it well. The senior executive can impart to these individuals his or her vision of how the dots should *probably* connect, in light of the organization's priorities and resources. This gives them enough to go on; it is part of their empowerment.

> **Empowerment means not just having the authority to do the job but also the appropriate knowledge and tools to do it well.**

While project leaders can be coerced into coordinating their efforts, the quality of their cooperation under that circumstance won't favor best outcomes. Empowering them to take leadership roles not only on their own turf but also in the larger mission of connecting the dots involves the calculated risk that, when they understand the senior executive's objectives, these high-initiative managers can achieve them and enhance them beyond expectation—in their own way. They will be, in a word, willing.

Their willingness depends on a number of factors:

- They need to understand the benefits to their project and to the organization of coordinated effort.
- They need to be confident that their contributions will be respected—that they are major architects of the more cohesive framework.

CONNECTING THE DOTS THROUGH A TECHNOLOGY STRATEGY

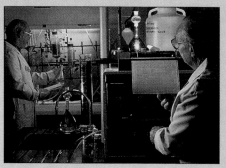

When this new chairman and CEO took over a $300 million organization serving the petroleum and industrial chemicals markets, he found a company in flux. Traditionally, a significant portion of the company's business had served domestic petroleum exploration and production companies. But massive changes were occurring in this market. Domestic oil production was shrinking as companies moved overseas to follow the oil giants' search for new production locations and a less hostile environmental setting. The CEO knew he needed to effect change—and quickly. He also knew the company's long tradition and bone-deep oil market culture would not make things any easier.

A number of change initiatives were under way at the time. They were of a kind you would recognize; many multinationals in the past decade have supported comparable programs. But the CEO and his senior associates knew that still more needed to be accomplished. The company had to rationalize and streamline its product offerings. Further, there was a shared recognition that future success would depend increasingly on the quality of customer service, not just on product quality. And in several areas they knew they needed to update substantially their business practices.

Each of these issues represented a potential improvement program. The CEO knew better than to launch them all independently.

Before assuming leadership, he had run a division where he witnessed the power of information technology as a lever for change. He had overseen the implementation of new systems and was impressed by the new think-

- They need to be certain of access to the tools, information, and resources that will make connecting the dots work and work well.
- They need the presence and availability of the senior executive to resolve disputes that are almost certain to arise.

Not every leader is willing to take on the challenge of empowering project leaders to become artisans of the larger integration the organization surely needs. The role is a delicate one: guiding but not too much, pushing but not too hard, being useful without being

ing that resulted from the implementation effort. Now, as CEO, he concluded the best way to force new thinking (and a common vision) across the company was to implement modern information systems. He knew the right systems would force constructive rethinking of business practices. Further, he believed a technology initiative could serve effectively as an umbrella for change efforts on a number of fronts. He decided to do it—and at warp speed.

The CEO commissioned a project to reshape the business practices and replace the entire portfolio of business systems in the company's North American operations. Hundreds of practices and more than 20 systems were to be replaced in 18 months—a very aggressive schedule. He was banking on the power of a difficult schedule to energize the change process, force a common vision, limit endless debate, and stimulate true out-of-the-box thinking.

He was right.

And to assure that things stayed on track, he attended many key project meetings to articulate—often—the ground rules:

No schedule changes.	No excuses.
No software modifications.	Get it done.

The positive structure provided by the functionality of the software, combined with this "take no prisoners" attitude and the urgent schedule, was just the right medicine. The process wasn't easy, but they got it done. The suite of application packages selected by the team "forced" the company to adopt up-to-date business practices. It lent structure to the various change initiatives. And the strong performance challenge of "get this done in 18 months" galvanized the team, focused them, and bonded them to a single overriding goal.

This was a change process in which the dots were connected both by executive decision and by the key structural concept that technology change could drive and unite other change efforts—an outstanding exercise.

tutorial. To bring together all of the energies for change in the organization and to reinvent positively how the organization operates, a leader needs other leaders who will not stop for advice and a fill-up every time they come around the track.

HOW TO CONNECT THE DOTS

It's your job to connect the dots. You've been tapped (or tapped yourself) to build or clarify the larger picture so that the mix of change projects at your company makes sense to those who staff them and for the organization as a whole. The challenge is nothing like making a one-off evaluation of the merits of any program and whether it does or does not represent a proper application of resources. The challenge is to evaluate and achieve program congruity. Do the programs, taken as a whole, powerfully reinforce a common vision? Or are there initiatives that pull the organization off track, off strategy?

Here are some steps you might take to start on this key evaluation:

1. Understand each program. We find that much conflict about change programs (be they TQM, reengineering, employee empowerment, or something else) is generated by those who have not been adequately informed or have not taken the time necessary to understand their rationale, methodology, and objectives. For the executive seeking to connect the dots, the following cures for this common situation should be considered:

> **Consider killing one or more programs that simply do not support the organization's goals. In any Darwinian pool of competitors, there are bound to be a few that just don't make it. So be it.**

a. **Meet with each program sponsor**. If you're on a mission that could shut down the program, expect the program sponsor to be on the defensive. Remember, then, that your first task is to understand, not to audit. The chances are good that there are plenty of positives. And you'll need the sponsor's support. Listen first. Make judgments later.

b. **List and reconcile each concurrent program's key rationale**. Identify the following for each program:

- Sponsor.
- Organization(s) or process(es) targeted for improvement.
- Change drivers (the "why" of the program).
- Key objectives (three to four brief statements).
- Methodology (again, three to four brief statements).
- Impact on the "levers of change," that is, the organization, human resources including reward systems, business processes and practices, and technology.
- Impact on customers.
- Life-cycle stage or time frame.

c. **Look for similarities before searching for differences**. This is important. Connecting the dots is often as simple as highlighting the congruence of what's going on. When you start by dissecting program goals, you are likely to find they have many goals in common as well as tactics for achieving them.

Two "Rights" Needn't Make a "Wrong"

Management of a major West Coast bank discovered two significant projects under way to improve performance in quite different functions. One, directed toward a service model, emphasized customer segmentation. Its rationale was that by segmenting customers more intelligently, the bank could better serve their special needs. The other project was directed toward giving those "closest to the customer" greater autonomy and empowerment. The latter team perceived itself as driving toward a more decentralized model—and perceived the former team as driving in the opposite direction, toward centralized modeling and service delivery.

As often happens, there was plenty of back-channel conflict that eventually erupted into open antagonism. Fortunately, senior management stepped in and connected the dots. They met with each team; understood its program; brought them together and rationalized a more truly joint approach that everyone perceived as a win.

2. Make choices. Once you have completed your analysis and formed careful conclusions, the time to act is *now*. Your choices are few, but important.

- Consider integrating teams. Ask project sponsors to share the best people, the vision, the effort, and the results. Realize that this may require concessions in leadership, project name, and many lesser issues.
- Consider discontinuing activities that have inadvertently or deliberately kept related programs apart.
- Consider killing one or more programs that simply do not support the organization's goals. In any Darwinian pool of competitors, there are bound to be a few that just don't make it. So be it.

3. Bury the dead (but not the wounded!). Recognize that some of your stakeholders believe in the program(s) you're about to kill. They will need to understand thoroughly the rationale for calling a halt to their group's activities. Unfortunately, projects or programs discontinued because they are perceived as failures can haunt an organization for years. At one of our clients, people still shiver at the mere mention of "Project Phoenix"—it has entered the realm of myth. It must have been a doozy! The point is that plenty of good people populate bad projects. The unit of employment is the

FIGURE 6.1
USING CUSTOMER FOCUS
TO CONNECT THE DOTS

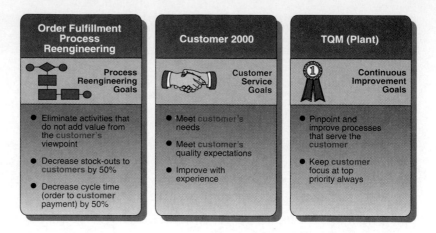

person, not the group. Good people furloughed from discontinued programs can find new organizational homes and become the stars they mean to be.

4. Resolve overlaps or conflicts. If you conclude (as you probably will) that several programs must continue on somewhat independent paths, and that merger is not in the organization's interest, you must clearly resolve any overlaps and conflicting messages. This is not necessarily an easy exercise, but it is an important one.

5. Connect the dots! Experience indicates that most of your programs will survive. It also indicates you won't be able to merge all that many of them into a single grand initiative. The task is to connect, not merge, the dots.

a. **Create the big picture for your audience**. Your best bet is to focus on the common themes in each program. Build a legitimate story of common change drivers, common objectives, similar tactics. Each program has its objective impact on the "levers of change." Use this ideology of levers of change to show how the parts fit the whole. Alternatively, or concurrently, build the common vision around customers. And look for similar lessons learned in each program.

b. **Draw a road map of yesterday and tomorrow**. Show the picture graphically (almost literally connect the dots) so that it is clear to everyone from the board of directors to entry-level professionals that what you are doing makes sense. Test out your map in places high and low, however, before you go public with it. Sometimes the obvious is not quite so obvious as we think.

An example of effective communication will be helpful. A CEO once created a giant visual map of all his company's major programs past and present. The document highlighted graphically and with text the programs carried out in the past and what had

One of our clients started an all-employee meeting by speaking as follows: "All of you are aware of the various programs and improvement initiatives we've undertaken in the past few years: total quality, employee involvement, learning organization, reengineering, and others. Many of you are wondering if these things fit together and if any of them has generated actual results. And you may be thinking, 'Why not just get back to the basics?'"

With these words, he acknowledged the doubt and cynicism in the workplace that he knew to be there. He then went on to discuss honestly the difficulties of implementing real change in a large organization and to reexplain the driving force behind all the company's initiatives. At that point he was ready to renew his call for action—and that's just what he did.

His presentation and its impact were wonders to behold. His honest assessment of what every employee already knew—that many of the programs were false starts, others poorly implemented—made him fully credible when he asked for renewed and better-integrated change efforts. By acknowledging candidly the successes and failures of the past and present, he prepared the employees to accept a vision of how the dots would connect in the future.

been learned from each. It linked these lessons to the rationale for today's programs. And it clearly communicated that there would be new programs tomorrow—in keeping with the company's commitment to functioning as a learning organization.

In broad strokes, the CEO's commentary on the map went something like this: "Five years ago we initiated our TQM program and learned the importance of serving customers (external and internal). We improved customer service, but let our costs get out of line. Our activity-based costing program, begun last year, is helping to cure this side effect. Through it, we are learning to control costs intelligently and focusing on better management of our horizontal processes. At present, we're beginning to reengineer those . . ." You see what sort of structure was developed.

> **Good people furloughed from discontinued programs can find new organizational homes and become the stars they mean to be.**

After absorbing this reasonably complex message, the employees of the organization were in a much better position to contribute their pieces to the solution of the puzzle. They understood the big

FIGURE 6.2
CONNECTING THE DOTS
USING CORE PROCESSES

One good way to connect the dots is to relate each of the initiatives currently under way to your core processes. Explain how each initiative supports one or more of these core processes and how they support each other.

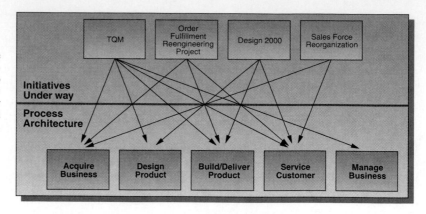

picture, the fit of one thing with another. The importance of working toward this understanding, and the productivity gains to be realized from it, cannot be overemphasized.

c. **Communicate the big picture plainly and effectively.** Employees love straight talk; bureaucrats love buzzwords, acronyms, and flowcharts that look like NASA wiring. One of our more seasoned practitioners puts his communications to the "mother/son test." If he cannot describe something so that his mother and his 10-year-old son can understand it, he tries again.

COMMUNICATE THE LEGITIMATE COMMON THEMES CLEARLY

Repeat the common themes over and over. Millions of dollars of research show that reinforcement is key to effective communication and belief. (The ad industry is built on this principle.) Remember, your listeners will hear and pick up any subtle changes in the message you send. Once you begin your campaign, keep the message clear and keep it consistent. A message deleted is heard more clearly than the message itself.

Before you launch your new program, look around you. Ask yourself how you can build upon the initiatives that exist currently. Reconcile yours to others to build understanding and collective momentum. It will pay.

Our metaphor of connecting the dots is drawn from a childhood game. Who hasn't been impressed by the exquisite concentration of a child connecting dots to discover a hidden picture? Something of that attitude is needed even in our adult corporate settings. Successfully connecting the dots among change programs calls for exquisite attention: to the real thrust of programs, to their fit, to their long-term impact, to the minds and feelings of their champions and staff.

CHECKLIST   CONNECTING THE DOTS

___ Understand each program. Meet with each program sponsor. List and reconcile each concurrent program's key rationales. Look for similarities before searching for differences.

___ Resolve overlaps and conflicts by making choices. Consider integrating teams, discontinuing disruptive activities, killing programs that don't support the overall goal. Communicate cancellations clearly and honestly, and be sure to find new organizational homes for good people coming off bad projects.

___ Connect the dots. Where multiple projects must continue somewhat independently, link them to each other via common change drivers, customers, objectives, tactics.

___ Show how current initiatives build on and fit with today's and tomorrow's programs. The linkage here is lessons learned and how this learning can be leveraged to improve performance continuously.

___ Communicate, communicate, communicate. Truthful, clear communication goes a long way toward solving the problems caused by program proliferation, and toward ending unnecessary proliferation. And nothing works better to refresh a jaded employee population.

SEVEN

Operating across Borders

T he modern corporation is a miracle of rational-ization. Each function managed by subject experts, each group of functions overseen by an experienced executive, each division directed by a senior executive, and so on up. This complex order represents for each company a tremendous heritage of know-how. However, the pressures of global competition are pointing up the flaws in the miracle. It is becoming clear that process reengineer-ing across departments provides critical efficiencies—and that the traditional corporate structure of impermeable borders tends to resist horizontal change efforts. This is a chapter about the risks and rewards of crossing those borders.

• • •

The sign at the international airport reads "Welcome," but you know better. What lies ahead is not warmth but formalities: certainly paperwork, perhaps delay and frustration. The borders between countries are intended to stop you, and they do so most efficiently. They subject you to at least minimal indignity as offi-cials look you over, and they make you pay in one way or another. If the border is particularly sensitive, you might not even make it past. It doesn't take much: a forgotten stamp in your passport that doesn't suit the local ideology, a harmless item in your luggage that excites interest, even something about your name.

In recent years, a number of seemingly permanent political and economic borders have been pierced or dismantled. On their own scale, borders within organizations can be just as enduring and troublesome as a Berlin Wall. Large-scale change projects typically encounter borders that bar the way forward, threaten to drain the change team's energy, and in worst case defeat the project. While most projects involve coordination among departments, divisions, or functions, companywide change projects are in a different league. They are broader in scope than typical operations improvement projects, and they tend to move over terrain for which the maps are old, misleading, or absent. Owing to their inherently horizontal orientation, change efforts tend to engage and affect many parts of the organization. In other words, they break through borders—often with mixed success.

BORDERS MATTER

Borders outline authority, power, responsibility. They provide perimeters for focused attention and accountability. No organization is without them. But by nature they impede change and can block it. They tend to limit opportunities to effect economies of scale, reduce redundancies, and optimize process efficiencies.

You can't reinvent your business without customer involvement. The borders of your enterprise are no more sacred than any of the internal borders you will encounter.

However, the solution to a problem in one functional area often lies somewhere past a border, in another functional area, and so borders are an issue. Years ago, a problem miles north of your division or a mile overhead at corporate headquarters might have been someone else's concern, not yours. But in broadbased change projects, there is no such isolation: *Mi casa es su casa* was never so meaningful. After determining that your problems are a function of what "they" do, you have to get "them" to do something about it.

As a change leader, you will need to be aware of borders and aware that crossing them successfully is critical to your success. You will be unable to ignore them. Even the best of companies with horizontally managed processes and a strong customer focus possess resistant internal borders. Despite that, they have learned how to encourage employees to serve the customer (not the boss) first. Discrediting and dismantling stubborn borders will not be easy. It will be rewarding.

CHAPTER SEVEN

TYPES OF BORDERS

Well, then, what borders? We have seen the following types in many, many companies:

• **Structural/organizational**. The most obvious borders are inherent to organizational structure. They may define departments, plants, divisions, and so on. Such units can be inflexibly bordered if they have a long history of fairly autonomous managerial control and if the reporting structure flows upward with few horizontal links.

• **Functional**. Borders around distinct functions (e.g., sales, finance, engineering, manufacturing) result from the American obsession with specialization as the key to efficiency. Business leaders are lately discovering that, while specialization may be efficient, it is not always effective. This organizational norm tends to pit accountants, engineers, manufacturing managers, sales personnel, against each other—although all serve the same enterprise and a common set of customers.

• **Cultural**. English has become the international language of business, but American customs and attitudes are not comparably universal. Cultural borders can be treacherous. Anyone who has facilitated dialogue on tough issues among participants representing such disparate cultures as the United States, Japan, Italy, and Mexico knows full well the complexities here. Think of the difficulty in solving problems when, for example, key foreign colleagues are accustomed to hedging because they think of hedging as polite, while you are accustomed to cutting through to decisions because you grew up in a business environment where incisive action was admired.

• **Language.** At a minimum, this border will slow you down. English may well be the language of global business, but subtleties are lost when nearly everybody around the table is speaking a second language.

• **Enterprise**. Change efforts may require you to go beyond the traditional borders of your organization. The input and cooperation of suppliers, strategic partners, and customers have become vital. You can't learn how to make these stakeholders happy if you don't know what's making them unhappy. You can't reinvent your business without customer involvement. The borders of your enterprise are no more sacred than any of the internal borders you will encounter.

• **Market**. Becoming more sophisticated as time goes on, market segmentation techniques deliberately create borders so that companies can focus on specific customer needs. However, there is also an internal impact: As your employees target discrete customer

FIGURE 7.1
BUILDING CHANGE
ACROSS BORDERS?
BETTER KNOW WHAT
YOU'RE UP AGAINST!

Rough translation:

1. Who commissioned this project? Did you know that in Europe our Engineering Group is way ahead on ISO 9000?

2. If I may not prejudge, however, in Japan, Mr. Sumi is moving Engineering under his control and...

3. Huh?

segments and serve them with passion, they can easily lose touch with the needs of the organization as a whole. Expect to hear: "You just don't understand our market."

• **Systems and technology**. Technologies create borders when differences exist in an organization's technology infrastructure. Dependence upon—or just as frequently, obsession with—disparate technologies can limit teamwork and cooperation.

WE'RE NOT MAKING TOO MUCH OF THIS

Borders can get pretty ugly. One of our consultants observed something during a business lunch hosted by the chief accounting officer of a major US corporation that can serve as an apt example. After being seated for lunch, the participants moved quickly past small talk to the tough issues faced by their host. Minutes later, the maître d' seated the company's CIO at the adjoining table. The chief accountant promptly leaned over and whispered that the discussion was *over* because the CIO was within earshot. He confided that this fellow was "the enemy." Their enmity was so strong, their differences of view so extreme, that he couldn't risk having his plans overheard. Forget about cooperation across their borders!

You may think that this situation could not occur in your own organization, but the statistics run against that pleasant likelihood. In 1991, the results of a *Harvard Business Review* survey led Michel Crozier to write:

FIGURE 7.2
AVERAGE PRODUCT
DEVELOPMENT CYCLE
TIMES WORLD

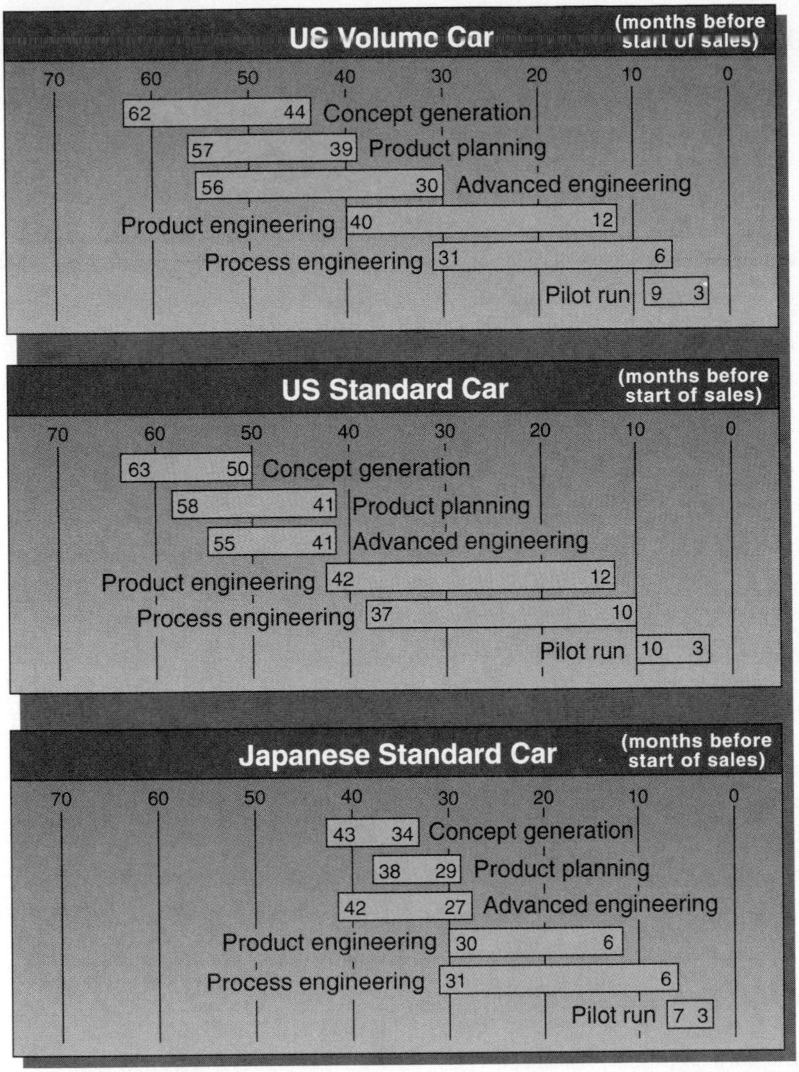

US Volume Car

(months before start of sales)

Phase	Start	End
Concept generation	62	44
Product planning	57	39
Advanced engineering	56	30
Product engineering	40	12
Process engineering	31	6
Pilot run	9	3

US Standard Car

(months before start of sales)

Phase	Start	End
Concept generation	63	50
Product planning	58	41
Advanced engineering	55	41
Product engineering	42	12
Process engineering	37	10
Pilot run	10	3

Japanese Standard Car

(months before start of sales)

Phase	Start	End
Concept generation	43	34
Product planning	38	29
Advanced engineering	42	27
Product engineering	30	6
Process engineering	31	6
Pilot run	7	3

Source: Adapted from Kim B. Clark and Takehiro Fujimoto, *Product Development Performance*, (1991).

Managers think their colleagues and employees now have a greater capacity to work in teams than they did 10 years ago. But there is an interesting difference between managers' judgments of their colleagues and their judgments of employees as a whole. Some 51 percent of respondents characterize employees as working well in teams today, while only 44 percent credit their managers with this ability.[1]

If only half of employees work well in teams, and somewhat less than half of the managerial ranks, little wonder that cross-border projects often go under.

[1] Michel Crozier, "The Boundaries of Business: Commentaries from the Experts," *Harvard Business Review*. July-August 1991, P. 138.

The competitive implications are significant. We often look to Japan for models or variants on our own practice. In this instance, Japan has long been heralded as the home of effective teamwork—and the truth of that claim is quantifiable. Figure 7.2 compares average product development cycle times in the global automobile industry. On average, Japanese car makers need 1.7 million engineering hours to develop a standard car compared with 3.2 million hours in the United States and 3 million hours for a volume car. Japanese mastery of the practice of simultaneous engineering is widely credited as the critical success factor in their high performance. In plain English, this means that the ability to get many departments, functions, skills sets, and geographic locations to operate in unison is the key to success.

GETTING IT DONE

Now that you have analyzed the borders facing you as you drive change in your organization, what must be done to make them work for you rather than against? Most traditional improvement projects have not involved the significant level of "border crossing" required by today's change projects. The new calculus of TQM, supplier partnering, customer focus, and particularly process reengineering have only recently enlightened managers to the significant benefits of rigorously integrating the activities across an organization's value chain. In the past, a strong orientation to hierarchical management and control naturally led to a greater number of change projects in which one had almost total control over those directly impacting and impacted by the project. Few cross-border muscles are developed in projects where you or your boss have such great influence over all the key stakeholders.

Most traditional improvement projects have not involved the significant level of "border crossing" required by today's change projects.

By their very nature, today's change projects cross many borders. Project sponsors cannot manage and control them in the traditional way. A different kind of manager is needed, neither exclusively vertical nor exclusively horizontal in his or her outlook. Such people are multidimensional thinkers who can envision and implement beneficial change across the matrix of departments and business units. The next section addresses this critical question of the change manager's identity and skills.

Cross-border solutions must be carefully crafted on the basis of innumerable factors native to the local situation, including local

CHAPTER SEVEN

strategies and customer and stakeholder needs. They cannot be taken off the shelf, replicated, and imposed where needed, nor can they be driven by the vision of someone in control who knows only his or her territory. We recently observed a successful change agent in a large manufacturing concern attempt to reproduce his magic in other areas of the company. All his experience, methods, and techniques were honed in manufacturing. He was quite surprised by the stiff opposition he received as he carried his methods to marketing, sales, and the finance and administrative functions. He had not taken the time to translate his message into their nomenclature. This heightened their normal skepticism, and his ideas were summarily rejected until he took the time to create a program much more tailored to their needs and circumstances. He succeeded by reducing his change program to its first principles and tying it to a one-page summary of the company's strategy. In this way his new audience could see it both in their terms and in light of the overall company's key objectives.

THE LEADERSHIP QUESTION

What kinds of individuals are needed to drive broad-based change projects in today's more global organizations? As Samuel Humes points out in his recent and engaging book titled *Managing the Multinational*:[2]

> While well-shared values and well-built structures are indispensable to coherent and competitive organizations, they are ineffective without managers who serve as the structural linchpins and culture carriers. The larger and more complex the organization, the more critical the management development process. Successful lateral as well as vertical collaboration, cross-border team efforts, and collegial styles at multiple levels rely upon a corps of managers who possess not only the requisite technical skills but also the interpersonal ones indispensable for teams sharing responsibility.

Unfortunately, most of today's project managers are not fully prepared to meet the demands of cross-border change efforts. Many don't have the experience to be effective. Their project experience has been gained in situations where they (or their superiors) wielded substantial influence or outright control over those involved in the effort and those directly affected by the changes. For this reason, they do not know the "feel" of the efforts and attitudes required to establish cross-border and companywide

[2] Samuel Humes, *Managing the Multinational* (Engelwood Cliffs, NJ: Prentice Hall, 1993), p. 365.

MUCH CHANGE—MANY BORDERS

Most reengineering projects deal with borders of one kind or another. Some focus on a process that crosses several functions (e.g., completing a month-end payroll run), while others work with linked processes often called a process chain (e.g., responding to a customer order). More rarely, reengineering projects address an entire enterprise and all its major process chains simultaneously. Many counsel that this is a recipe for disaster. Bite off a piece at a time, they say—walk before you run.

A major US-based producer of chemicals put all the caveats aside. The risk of not performing large-scale reengineering at once and within a short time frame was perceived to be the greatest risk of all. As it turned out, the gamble paid off—handsomely.

The company began its reengineering from an all-too-familiar starting point: the end of an unprecedented period of success. Two years earlier, the company had been almost the most profitable in its industry. Now, red ink was flowing, largely due to shifting market conditions and lower market prices for its primary products. A new CEO was convinced that something drastic was needed to restore the company to health. As he put it, the company had "caught pneumonia, and we need some penicillin."

The "medicine" recommended was a complete reengineering of its three business units, including operations and facilities on three continents. The time frame to define the new blueprint—six months. No function or process was to be spared the reengineering scalpel: R&D, marketing and sales, finance and control, customer order management, production, planning and logistics were all targeted. In an impressive way, the team chose to overwhelm the borders within the organization. By setting such a comprehensive scope, the company was virtually forced to overcome its barriers to change.

How were boundaries overcome? To manage this behemoth task, the project was broken into logical process chains addressed by separate teams. Frequent border checks were conducted to manage and pass key design assumptions back and forth across the interfaces between these process chains. The task was large. At one point, over 500 people out of a 4,000-person work force were actively involved in the reengineering effort.

The comprehensive scale of this effort had the benefit of avoiding a problem that can develop in many change projects of lesser scope where root causes outside the target area must be queued up for subsequent analysis and disposition. Because everything was in play, these issues could be dealt with in a timely and holistic fashion and the resultant new process and organizational design did not have many dangling loose ends that had to be dealt with after the fact.

By changing long-standing assumptions and procedures regarding how plants were scheduled and loaded, substantial manufacturing efficiencies and inventory reductions were attained, as well as quality improvements and material-waste cost savings.

On the speed dimension, overall responsiveness increased by 75 percent, as quantified by a broad range of measures including time to commercialize new products and customer response time. The sources of these speed improvements were the application of JIT concepts to the R&D labs and process plants, establishment of customer response teams, redefined planning processes, and streamlined approvals.

Most of the improvements required little or no systems support at the early stage. On the other hand, many will require systems enhancements to sustain continuous improvement. Some systems (e.g., a new interplant scheduling and product loading optimization system) were developed and implemented in just a few months. More complex systems such as integrated MRP and reporting systems will require one to two years to implement fully.

The dividends from this effort were not only material and quantifiable. There were some intangibles. By successfully tackling such a comprehensive reengineering project, the company experienced a dramatic change in self-perception. It gained confidence in its ability to heal itself—and full recovery is expected. Although many of the long-term benefits have yet to be attained, achieving the short-term goals has given employees a new vigor. The long-term benefits can be expected to add to and magnify the success to date.

When the new vision has been fully implemented, combined results are projected to yield over $50 million in annual savings, plus a onetime savings of $100 million in inventory and railcar storage costs. These are major gains. The company expects to restore its market leadership.

FIGURE 7.3
YESTERDAY'S MANAGERS
Mostly "vertical" management
skills.

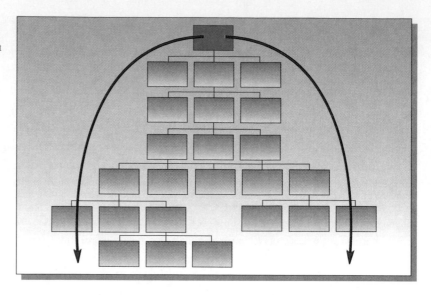

coalitions that generate balanced solutions. Even the best project
managers have typically developed what one might call "vertical
muscles." In facing horizontal, organizationwide change efforts,
they will need to inspire and motivate project team members,
influence stakeholders, and exercise their political savvy in ways
almost certainly not encountered in the past.

Companies will need to look for people with the skills and
experience necessary for this task. Since the appropriate experience
will not be in many people's portfolios, you will probably need to
make educated guesses as to who will best learn from the effort
and mature in the leadership role as it develops. "Savvy" is the
critical trait; it cannot be quantified, but you can recognize when
a manager has the right combination of intelligence, experience,
courtesy, and force. Your change leaders will need to be capable
of thinking along process lines. They will have a strong customer
service bias. They will be smart enough to see what is going on

FIGURE 7.4
TOMORROW'S MANAGERS
Wide influence across "horizontal"
organizations.

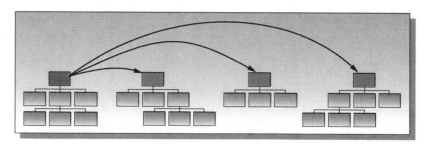

CHAPTER SEVEN

around them—for example, to see that not everyone absorbs change in the same way and at the same rate, and that other worthy project participants may legitimately perceive problems and opportunities differently than they do. They will respect the fact that decisions they make will affect the fortunes of the entire enterprise, but this impact will neither paralyze them nor turn them into egomaniacs. Well-devised plans to carry out change do not circumvent the need for such savvy managers who can propagate the new vision and see to its implementation throughout the enterprise.

"Savvy" is the critical trait; it cannot be quantified, but you can recognize when a manager has the right combination of intelligence, experience, courtesy, and force.

Finding, grabbing, and holding on to a first-class project manager is critical—but no more critical than the structure of the project team itself. We classify project teams into three types. The team structure depicted in Figure 7.5 reflects the "throw it over the wall" mentality. Each function provides a representative to work jointly on the project. However, no strong project manager exists, and coordination is assumed to be in the hands of the four functional bosses under the guidance of the sponsor. For simple projects that require only the sequential input of functional perspectives, this structure may suffice. However, the structure is vastly unsuited to addressing complex problems that require tight project management.

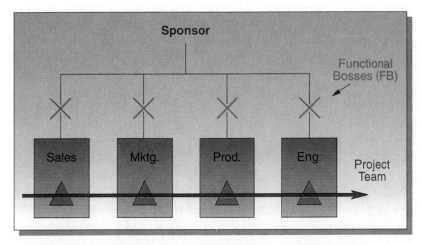

FIGURE 7.5
FUNCTIONAL TEAM
STRUCTURE

Source: Adapted from K. Clark and S. Wheelwright, "Organizing and Teaching Heavyweight Development Teams," *California Management Review*, Spring 1992.

FIGURE 7.6
LIGHTWEIGHT TEAM
STRUCTURE

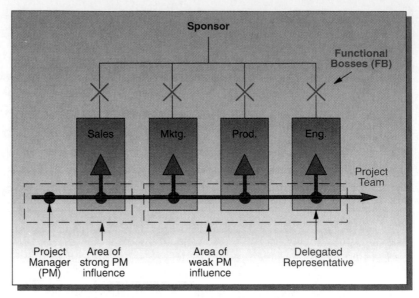

Source: Adapted from K. Clark and S. Wheelwright, "Organizing and Teaching Heavyweight Development Teams," *California Management Review*, Spring 1992.

The second structure (Figure 7.6), the lightweight team, addresses this project management weakness. A project manager is appointed to encourage teamwork, set deadlines, and monitor deliverables. However, the presence of this project manager often leads each of the functions to reduce its level of commitment and to appoint a junior representative to sit on the team. An additional difficulty involves the project manager's reporting line: If he or she is drawn from one of the functions involved, such as sales, and continues to report to that functional boss, the project manager may have only a weak influence on the other functional representatives.

The heavyweight (Figure 7.7) structure really delivers. The project manager is a senior, well-respected individual. He or she is released from the functional reporting structure and reports directly to the sponsor. Further, any attempt to delegate responsibility to junior representatives is rebuffed. Experience shows this type of team to be ideal for managing complex, multifunctional change projects.

START WITH THE CUSTOMER

In looking for ways to build consensus and momentum, you will do well to start by crossing the enterprise border and talking with customers. They are the common denominator; they figure in everybody's equations—or should. The fundamental drive to serve cus-

CHAPTER SEVEN

FIGURE 7.7
HEAVYWEIGHT TEAM
STRUCTURE

Sponsor

Functional
Bosses (FB)

| Sales | Mktg. | Prod. | Eng. |

Project
Team

Project
Manager
(PM)

Area of
strong PM
influence

Delegated
Representative

Source: Adapted from K. Clark and S. Wheelwright, "Organizing and Teaching Heavyweight Development Teams," *California Management Review*, Spring 1992.

tomers is so much in everybody's best interest that it can become almost a basic instinct. If this is not the situation in your company, your customers will tell you. Look for ways to rally change around customer needs.

BUILD COALITIONS

In planning the scope of a change project, it is critically important to build the proper coalitions among the various units involved, with all constituents' views represented on the project team. The time needed to build coalitions and consensus must be budgeted at significant levels. In our experience, no one ever overestimates the

time required. The project manager in a comprehensive change project typically spends more than half of his or her time working—mostly across borders—to build unanimity of view and support for change. To this purpose, organizational and political skills are as important as technical skills. We always recommend that a well-respected line execu-tive serve as the sponsor of a significant change project.

In looking for ways to build consensus and momentum, you will do well to start by crossing the enterprise border and talking with customers.

Co-locating resources can help build coalitions. The explosion at the World Trade Center in the winter of 1993 left a cavernous wound in the operational heart of many organizations. In addition to the physical and emotional harm done, it was also an economic disaster of significant proportion for many. Trade Center managers recognized this and knew they had to mount an extraordinary effort to get the building back on line. In an environment in which heavy construction seems to move at a glacial pace, it did not look promising. Beyond the enormity of the physical work to be done, coordinating the efforts of dozens of independent organizations made the problem seriously daunting.

As soon as your change team begins to meet, openly identify barriers that you know will slow the change effort. If possible, dismantle them, but at least deal with them.

What ensued was a remarkable example of what is possible when borders don't exist. The business and government officials heading the cleanup and reconstruction effort mounted an awesome campaign—well managed and highly orchestrated. The effort was praiseworthy in many respects. What we found most interesting was the way in which they brought all the necessary security, clean-up, engineering, and construction resources together into an immense war room setting. Co-location became their main ally in dismantling any and all barriers between organizations working to clean up and reconstruct the building. The project made extraordinary progress because dozens of organizations were encouraged and managed to think and act like one.

Horizontal Chunks

If you find stiff resistance to change, try the pilot or prototype approach by making a significant change in a narrowly focused but important process. Encouraged by a positive "portable" success in this pilot effort, you can move on with greater confidence to the next work site elsewhere in the organization. One of our clients is reengineering and rationalizing the procurement aspects of its worldwide supply chain. The company has adopted the approach of getting it right first in the United States—or at least showing significant improvements. Then and only then will the company attempt to implement its new business model, encompassing organization, technology, and processes, in Europe, Asia, and South America. This approach will then be repeated for core processes other than the supply chain. We call this technique effecting change "in horizontal chunks."

In using this technique, you may want to keep things relatively loose, informal, and quiet, penetrating barriers and implementing change in almost guerrilla fashion. Why "go public" with a successful change effort until you have proof positive of its good results? This slight stealth may help to disarm old line, hierarchical defenders of their borders, who would be put on alert to strengthen their defenses if you were to announce a frontal assault. Instead, gradually encircle the "enemy." When you have shown several times what you can accomplish in friendlier territory, the "enemy" may voluntarily lower the draw-bridge and invite you in.

VERTICAL CHUNKS

An alternative strategy of proven value is to take comprehensive change as your initial objective, but to limit the effort to a single business unit. Driving change in a single business unit (for example, a division or plant) makes the project more manageable, with a greater possibility of success. If and when you achieve visible success, roll out the change program to other units. You might choose, for example, to implement a comprehensive total quality program in your European division. When the good results begin to take shape, there is time enough to introduce the process to divisions in other parts of the world. We call this approach effecting change "in vertical chunks." In all likelihood, you will probably settle on a combination of these two strategies by addressing both vertical and horizontal elements as you prove the value of your change program to all concerned and gain their buy-in.

BE ANALYTIC; BE SPECIFIC

As soon as your change team begins to meet, openly identify barriers that you know will slow the change effort. If possible, dismantle them, but at least deal with them. As in many other arenas of life, once you understand the nature of the beast, you know more than a little about how to slay it. We know of one very experienced change agent who, after he has crystallized a vision of the contemplated changes, writes in very plain English on a large "white board" in the project war room every major barrier the team expects to encounter. The statements include things such as: "Creative's unwillingness to deal with the new requisition process" or "Operations not getting us the well data until three days after close" or "Business heads not giving us their time." By doing this, he forces the team (and the broader, more senior project steering committee) to face the reality of the obstacles ahead. They are continually reminded of the specific cross-border solutions that must be negotiated to achieve their objectives. This is often the toughest work in a change effort. He wants it right there in front of them all the time.

ENHANCING COMPETITIVENESS THROUGH A BORDER STRATEGY

Social, economic, and legislative factors were exerting intense pressure on a major international entertainment and media concern owned in part by a government. Despite its deserved reputation for technical and professional excellence, its funding was not guaranteed and its income was tied to the rate of inflation. Until now, its main concern had been to carry out its work to the highest possible standards and keep costs within budget. But now it was having to fight to retain its business. The organization was asked to equip itself, within a very short time, with a new structure and set of skills to carry out a whole series of operations with which it was essentially unfamiliar.

Initial evaluation of the organization and its problems indicated the culture needed serious reorientation if the new challenges were to be successfully addressed. The decision was made to start the change process in one department and to let the results there serve not only as a process model for getting other work done but also as proof that well-conceived, well-managed change in this organization was compatible with preserving the company's reputation for quality.

The change team decided to start in the film department, but not directly within the department. They worked the border. The organization's entertainment and media producers were given a new choice: They could use the internal resources on which they had relied in the past, including the film department, or go into the marketplace for competitively priced quality resources.

The impact of this new option on the film department was immediate: The department

Another manager we know gets his team to write down what those cross-border stakeholder groups value. For example, with regard to cultural borders, he might get his group members to ask themselves: Do they favor rigorous market research? Or is "Quick, get the product to market!" at the top of their agendas? The sooner you put these things down on paper and get them in front of your team, the better off you will be. Dealing with them is the only way to move ahead.

BE BOLD

A technique valued by the executives we know who show flair in this area of management involves continually pressuring the borders by operating as if they do not exist and never asking permission to cross them. These men and women just move on through on now had to compete for business from the organization's producers as if it were an outside vendor. This was a very powerful agent of change: Yesterday you waited for the phone to ring, the work came to you automatically. Today the phone may never ring again.

Obviously, this was not just an issue for the film group. The producers were freed to make comparable buy/make decisions concerning financial systems, human resources development, and marketing. While the film department was second to none in quality production, its professionals were not practiced in putting themselves in the customer's frame of mind. Developing internal vendor/customer relationships forced them to consider a range of questions for the first time. What services did their customers want? How could they best offer them? How could they retain business in competition with the external market and still keep within budget?

Once these priority questions were identified, change plans could emerge that had a real chance of success. The film department's management team was involved wholeheartedly from the start. Through their enthusiasm over the possibilities, they won over the hearts and minds of those who would be most affected by and ultimately have to implement change.

News of the initial success of the film department project spread quickly throughout the enterprise. Analogous change programs based on putting the crucial make/buy decision in the hands of the producers are now being rolled out in other departments.

the assumption that, were they to ask permission to cross a border, someone with clout would answer no. They do not always succeed; the technique is not without its casualties. On the other hand, when they do succeed, they contribute tremendously to the development of a new operating reality within their organizations, based on horizontal processes and interdepartmental teamwork.

KNOW YOUR LIMITS

The possible rewards of a change project increase exponentially with the number of "border crossings." The same must be said, however, of the attendant risks. The danger of biting off more than you (or the project sponsor) can chew must be kept in mind. It will be important to stay within the political reach of the executive sponsor. If you cross key borders without the strength to do so,

FIGURE 7.8
UNDERSTANDING PROJECT
COMPLEXITY

As scope increases horizontally and borders are crossed (generally a positive thing), project complexity, project risk, and the potential rewards of the change effort increase at an accelerating rate.

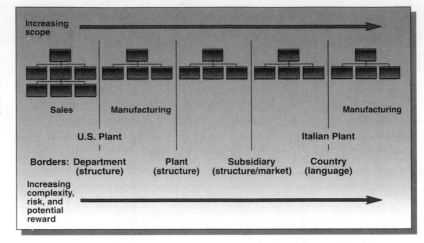

your recommendations may be repelled by stronger political foes. This is a sorry fate. We recommend: Be bold. We also recommend: Know your limits. A rule of thumb may help here. In setting scope, try writing down the borders crossed in a project scope that is comfortably within the change sponsor's sphere of influence. Then ask yourself: Will it be beneficial to cross yet one more border?

> **Much energy can go to waste if management passes lightly over the issue of who has decision rights in cross-border change projects.**

This is the tack taken by a change team at a manufacturer we know. The change sponsor wanted to streamline and better integrate all the activities that made up the procurement process. He believed, with the support of the plant manager, that he could drive change at his plant and at corporate headquarters. Wanting to push the envelope, he decided to include a sister plant. It was a stretch—with the risk of slowing down his project. But he knew the benefits would be more than doubled, were both plants to undertake this effort. This more than doubled the time he needed to spend communicating and working with stakeholders. On the other hand, significant synergy developed as the two plants worked on the project together.

BE CLEAR ABOUT "DECISION RIGHTS"

Recognizing that borders exist is the first step; analyzing the nature and dynamics of harmful borders is the second step; acting thereafter as if they don't exist is the third step. But behind this bold third step there must be a carefully calculated plan, the right combination of authority and responsibility, and an awareness of where the real limits lie. Much energy can go to waste if management passes lightly over the issue of who has decision rights in cross-border change projects. We observed a team from a division of a major food processor wading through a 12-month change planning project, spending much money and much time. At least monthly, the change team members met with corporate staff and other "cross-border" authorities to report and test their thinking. But it was never clear in these meetings what authorities were being afforded the team and its sponsor (the division head).

The team finally reached important conclusions as to where and how the company would make major investments to upgrade operations only to be told by the corporate executive group that the team was not empowered to make those decisions. Had this been clear at a much earlier stage—had the decision rights been debated and understood by all—extensive time and effort could have been saved.

PUT A KEY EXECUTIVE IN CHARGE OF EACH KEY BUSINESS PROCESS

Every company has at most four or five basic business processes (e.g., order fulfillment, procurement, product development, R&D). While very few companies will completely reorganize along process lines, a single highly placed executive should have the overall responsibility of "getting it done" with respect to each key business process—regardless of the borders crossed by that process as it moves through the organization. Such an executive rarely has line authority over all process resources, but he or she is usually senior enough and respected enough to wield the necessary influence. This is not a role for thin-skinned folks. The best process champions are tactful but tenacious.

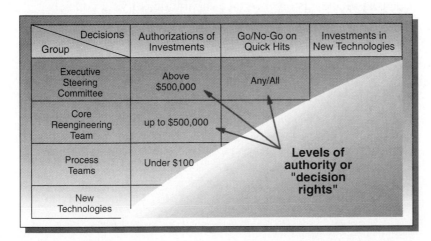

FIGURE 7.9
FORMALIZING DECISION RIGHTS

To promote a powerful bias for action, empower your teams and spell out clearly their level of authority.

Know the People "Over There"

To be effective in creating change across a border, find out all you can about the people who make their professional lives on the other side, whether this means "the folks in accounting" or "the plant managers" or "the guys in our French operation." Getting to know your cross-border associates isn't difficult, once you show interest and some knowledge concerning the things that matter to them. Specifically regarding cross-cultural borders, books such as Johnson and Moran's *Cultural Guide to Doing Business in Europe*[3] can be very helpful. For example, the following are points from Moran's short list of dos and don'ts with French colleagues and business partners:

- Be prompt.
- Don't use toothpicks, combs, or nail clippers in public.
- Shake hands with a single, quick shake.
- When ending a visit, wait for a polite silence before rising.
- "Dropping in" is inappropriate; wait to be invited or telephone ahead to apprise people of your plans.
- Respect the French notion of "business secrecy."

While ignoring these customs is unlikely to crater your project, inadvertently creating irritation by your manner is no way to secure cooperation.

Dismantle Those Borders

Ultimately, borders will need to be replaced by seamless organizations. Issues of cultural differences, market nuances, and the like are important but peripheral to the central issue of the internal organization and customer service capabilities of your company. For many companies, survival will depend on developing the kind of "boundarylessness" that is already characteristic of a few major—and massively successful—US multinationals.

Peter Drucker, dean of American management consultants, surely sees the future with great clarity when he writes:

> The typical large business 20 years hence will have fewer than half the levels of management of its counterpart today, and no more than a third the managers. In its structure, and in its management problems and concerns, it will bear little resemblance to the typical manufacturing company, circa 1950, which our textbooks still consider the norm. Instead it is far more likely to

---

[3] Michael Johnson and Robert T. Moran, *Cultural Guide to Doing Business in Europe* (Oxford: Butterworth-Heinemann, 1992), p. 53.

resemble organizations that neither the practicing manager nor the management scholar pays much attention to today: the hospital, the university, the symphony orchestra. For, like them, the typical business will be knowledge-based, an organization composed largely of specialists who direct and discipline their own performance through organized feedback from colleagues, customers, and headquarters.

Traditional departments will serve as guardians of standards, as centers for training and the assignment of specialists; they won't be where the work gets done. That will happen largely in task-focused teams.[4]

> **Issues of cultural differences, market nuances, and the like are important but peripheral to the central issue of the internal organization and customer service capabilities of your company.**

Take action now.

We have not quite managed to say yet that there is a good deal of joy and professional satisfaction in working toward the borderless organization. Every good business manager has an artisan's interest in how things work, and how they can work better. Change projects across borders will provide much insight along these lines. Almost every good business manager we know also has two goals: to make lots more money and to have his or her proudest management initiative written up as a Harvard Business School case study. Change projects across borders are at the leading edge of management today. They can help you toward both goals.

CHECKLIST OPERATING ACROSS BORDERS

___ Be aware of the borders your change must cross to work.
   ___ Structural/organizational
   ___ Functional
   ___ Enterprise
   ___ Markets
   ___ Cultural
   ___ Systems and technology
   ___ Language
___ Find the right change managers. Look for savvy leaders and those with potential who are
   ___ Intelligent, experienced, courteous and forceful.
   ___ Capable of thinking along process lines.

[4] Peter F. Drucker, "The Coming of the New Organization," *Harvard Business Review*, January/February 1988, p. 22.

___ Biased strongly toward customer service.

___ Able to consider the needs of other stakeholders in the change, but not paralyzed by them.

___ Assemble a coalition project team from across borders; make sure the leader is sufficiently savvy, well known, and senior to earn cross-border respect.

___ Co-locate the project team physically (put them in a room together) or logically (give them communications technologies that enable them to work together as though in the same room).

___ Cross the enterprise border immediately, and enlist the voice of the customer in your change effort.

___ Work in chunks. Use a successful pilot change in one geographic, functional, or process area to sell your approach in the next.

___ Identify specific borders and barriers early and often. Publish them to the team; post them in your war room. Get everyone's ideas and contacts into play about how to best dismantle or cross borders.

___ Consider operating as though there were no borders. It's risky, but can be the fastest, most inspiring route to a new reality.

___ Know your limits so that you know when you are incurring additional risk. Understand the nature and dynamics of dangerous border crossings before the attempt.

___ Get clarity on decision rights. Have clear scope and authority with which to make change happen. This will preempt many minor border battles.

___ Put a senior executive with tact and tenacity in charge of business processes.

___ Know the people on the other side of the border. Understand their culture and their wins. That will help you to avoid unnecessary irritation or errors, which might damage your bid to cross their border. If they can see what you see, they may help you dismantle the border, which is the ultimate goal.

Thinking Big, Acting New

T hinking big and acting new are high on the agenda of US corporate leaders. But these values will remain agenda items and have little impact without a practical approach that converts the creativity and courage of employees into agreed plans and timetables for change. This chapter takes you through a proven approach to thinking big, acting new—and making it all work in the real world. One key element is a diversified change team that, far from groping for a method, knows how to go about its business. Another key element is a companywide "tryout" that challenges and refines big ideas, earns buy-in, and creates readiness to implement. The third key element is you—your own belief in the need to think big and act new, your ability to communicate that belief infectiously and stand by it even when cries and whispers across the organization cause others to stand back.

• • •

In the early days of the mainframe computer, some industry leaders believed that in time there would be just a handful of giant computers attending to the computing needs of the world. Surprisingly enough, the same thinking was current in the early days of the personal and home computer industry. Some well-placed people believed that sooner or later there would be a very powerful computer in your home, serving both your household management and home computing needs. We suspect there must have been someone involved in the development of the electric motor whose thinking was similarly monolithic. Just imagine this chap, wiping the grease from his hands as he sat back and envisioned the future: a single huge electric motor, perhaps in your basement (with pulleys and v-belts spinning in all directions), supplying power to your refrigerator, washing machine, dishwasher, lawn mower . . .

Innovation isn't easy. As these examples illustrate, it isn't even easy to envision how new ideas will be applied in the future. But innovation—thinking big ideas, acting on new ideas—must be one of your objectives as you drive change through your organization. There is no healthy alternative.

We have written this chapter in response to the concern frequently expressed by senior executives that they do not find enough innovative thinking in their organizations. The rewards for innovation, they know, are immense in today's world economy. As the world becomes a global market, the leverage provided by a big idea taken worldwide is enormous. Further, these executives know that their competitors, driven by the same vision of the global market, are ceaselessly pressing for new ideas.

Few breakthroughs materialize. The reason for this is not hard to find: Significant innovation is a product of embedded corporate culture, not a fast-food item.

Under these conditions, the idea of evolving into "a learning organization" emerges as something more than an attractive slogan. It becomes an imperative: learn, change, or fall behind. Responding to this imperative, companies initiate change projects and seek out big ideas. But the level of effort and investment committed by organizations to reinventing themselves doesn't often square with the level of results achieved. There is talk about "breakthrough" ideas and thinking "out of the box." At the end of the day, however, few really big ideas are surfaced; few startling performance breakthroughs are achieved. Or so it seems. This disappointment causes managers to start looking for "the next program" promising a shortcut to success. And the process repeats itself.

The creativity that could and should be stirring within organizations is often needlessly constrained, owing to a pair of misconceptions concerning innovation. Some companies simply do not focus on innovation; they fail to perceive it as the key to survival and growth. Other companies take an unnecessarily narrow view of innovation by focusing strictly on scientific innovation—R&D. Because they aren't looking in other directions, they miss opportunities for process innovation, business practice innovation, human resources innovation, communications innovation—and more.

So, despite a stream of brochures, seminars, and programs promising "breakthrough" concepts and eye-popping business improvement, few breakthroughs materialize. The reason for this is not hard to find: Significant innovation is a product of embedded corporate culture, not a fast-food item. Savvy managers who worry about the imbalance between heavy effort and light results want to understand better how to foster meaningful innovation and change processes, and how to build into the corporate culture the values and practices that make breakthroughs more likely.

BEGIN WITH BELIEVING

There will not be much big thinking if your people don't believe that change—big change—is imperative. At the beginning of a change-related assignment, we often survey the organization, asking employees and focus groups what they think about change. Typically, there is a modicum of agreement regarding the need to change. But when you ask people *how much* change is necessary (for example, on a scale of 1 to 10), responses vary dramatically. Seldom is there consensus about the required magnitude of change.

There are so many reasons not to change. By nature, change is uncomfortable, stressful, threatening. All of us benefit by the wisdom we have accumulated—and change often makes that wisdom of less value to the organization. As a consequence, we fear we won't be able to adapt, won't prove to be a learning cell in a learning organization. In view of all this, you must convince your people that change is imperative and it will make a positive difference for each and all. If they fail to see the possibilities in front of them—cannot at least imagine that things could be different and better—then you cannot expect meaningful change to occur. (See Chapter Two, "Building the Case for Change.")

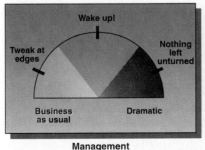

Management

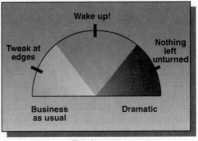

Employees

FIGURE 8.1
THE CHANGE METER TEST
Consider a simple survey. Ask your managers how much change is needed. Then ask your employees. Notice any difference?

A Culture, a Mind-set

Innovation—thinking big, thinking new—is an important constituent of the culture of successful organizations. It is a strong, highly valued characteristic in world-class companies. On the other hand, in companies something less than world class, floating new and radical ideas is subtly, although never openly, discouraged. In such organizations, the risk/reward trade-off is steeply canted toward risk aversion. If new ideas are not valued and the reaction to failure is essentially punitive, there is no motive to create and promote big, new ideas.

The degree to which innovation is valued can vary widely even within organizations. For example, in consumer product manufacturing companies, you would expect the new product development groups to be replete with innovators. On the other hand, how many would you expect to find in Payroll, in Purchasing, in Maintenance? Innovators are needed *throughout* the organization, but the managers of these departments will never know whether their people have "the right stuff" if the departments' unspoken values militate against innovative thinking.

High-performance organizations always place great value upon new ideas. Their senior executives view themselves as building an organization characterized by continuous change. Innovation is the fuel of the change process. One of the important reasons for employee-involvement and continuous-improvement programs is to promote the value of new ideas. As Roger von Oech reminds us in his book, *A Whack on the Side of the Head*, "Nothing is more dangerous than an idea when it's the only one you have."[1] He's absolutely right. It doesn't matter how well you're doing now. Count on two truths: first, your competitors are working to do it better; second, it *can* be done better.

In the next case study, a fast-growing, highly profitable electronics firm—experiencing major growing pains and blaming it all on product codes—starts thinking big, thinking new.

Foster Innovation in the Change Process

The kind of innovation required by performance improvement projects is unusual. In our experience, fostering and harnessing creativity should be central to large-scale organizational change. This requires you to engage people's imaginations as well as their innate desire to improve their lot in life (see Chapter Three, "Motivating Stakeholders"). In addition, the process must inspire

[1] Roger von Oech, *A Whack on the Side of the Head* (Menlo Park, CA, Creative Think, 1992), p. 26.

individuals and, ultimately, groups to coordinate their actions and decisions in new ways. The challenge is not to "invent something and we'll see if it's meaningful to the business." The challenge is to generate BIG change—truly significant, bottom-line performance improvement.

A step-change in performance requires big thinking about customers, markets, processes, and technologies. Processes don't think; organizations don't conceive; technologies don't act. Only your people can think big thoughts; only they can innovate. They can act anew, reinventing the business as it can and should be today.

Persuading the organization to *act new* is not a small thing. It means getting lots of people—perhaps everyone up, down, and across the organization—to accept responsibility for changing the fundamentals of their individual organizational roles. A tall order—but it can be accomplished, and accomplished methodically. If and when you succeed, you will have achieved what is without doubt the most sustainable performance improvement of all. A new organizational structure is fine. New technology may help you leapfrog competitors—until they leapfrog you and the cycle begins again. But nothing can match an organization filled with highly motivated, highly innovative people. This is an unassailable advantage, as Herb Kelleher and the people of Southwest Airlines have learned in the case on page 158.

> **Processes don't think; organizations don't conceive; technologies don't act. Only your people can think big thoughts; only they can innovate.**

Southwest Airlines and other successful organizations have achieved major change by harnessing the creativity of their employees. You can, too. Here are principles to bear in mind when embarking on a change project in which you need your people to be innovative. Applying these principles sensibly is the surest way to catalyze thinking big, acting new.

THE CHANGE TEAM: INNOVATION THROUGH DIVERSITY

Innovation depends on first exploring and then integrating diverse and unconventional points of view. Too many change committees are comprised of seven or eight 45-year-old white males who have been with the company for 23 years. We're certainly not suggesting that people meeting these demographics have nothing to offer. We do suggest that a more diverse group is more likely to generate the "out-of-the-box" thinking so fundamental to creative solutions in the change process.

OVERCOMING CONVENTIONAL WISDOM

The whole problem resulted from improper product codes. Right? It seemed to people in the organization that whenever they didn't have the right product available for a customer, there was a product-code problem at the root of it. Or when they needed to know the status of an order and had difficulty, the cause of the difficulty was the infamous product code. Like much conventional wisdom that bends reality to its own shape, product coding was the universal explanation. And this "fact" discouraged new thinking about other sources of difficulty—and possible fixes.

In reality, the codes *were* an issue, but the business processes that had grown up around product codes were the actual root of the company's problems. Marketing and Sales were frustrated by the time it took to move a variation of a product into the commercial system. As a consequence, they often had to bootleg products to meet customers' needs. Cost Accounting was taking months to develop costs for each product variation (and there were about 500 per year). Engineering was no less frustrated—department members were convinced they spent all their time getting signatures and developing bills of materials. Only 80 percent of the company's shipments were on time, despite high inventory levels. And determining product availability was nearly impossible.

An effective change sponsor picked up the reins. He first persuaded the organization to stop focusing on a single issue and, instead, examine the larger business model of serving customers. Process reengineering was initiated with the aim of improving dramatically the company's ability to respond to customers. The entire customer-response chain of processes was reviewed, as were cost

The goal is to involve your change team in one of the most important ways of "thinking big." Something we call *linked innovation* occurs when experienced but open-minded players coming from many parts of the organization and shaped by different professional backgrounds work together. They will bring individual, diverse perspectives to the facts before them. Recognizing that not everyone is creative, you will want to include in the team your company's savviest risk takers and broad-gauge thinkers, and this almost certainly means ignoring titles and levels to some noticeable degree. All of the seemingly faddish talk about the value of nonhierarchical management structures becomes a working reality here. You may be surprised how naturally seniors and subordinates of comparable ability learn to team when properly inspired and motivated.

accounting and the administrative functions of product development. Approximately 40 processes were analyzed. A team of about 25 keen-minded people received training in process design and then set about redesigning the business processes in and around customer service.

Some highlights of their results include:

- Universal identifiers, understood by everyone, replaced product codes. Product variations can now be added to "commercial systems" in a day versus a month (for product codes) and with about 80 percent lower resource requirements.
- Scheduling can now react to changes in demand on a daily basis, versus a two-week basis, with less than half the resources previously required.

- A major change in policy reduced the number of times product costing needed to be done: down to 20 from 500 per year.
- Lag in responding to customer inquiries has been reduced from the previous one-to-two-day interval to about 15 minutes.
- Most of the 40-plus processes reengineered are now on average 75 percent faster and require 35 percent fewer resources. The savings amounts to the equivalent of about 40 full-time people, all of whom were absorbed through business growth and reassignment to customer value-adding tasks.

A big win from thinking big, acting new. None of this would have been accomplished had the company not been thinking new.

Assembling your best and brightest is not enough. You must provide them with a common performance objective. Nothing is more important to team performance than strong shared commitment to a common goal. Make them all accountable for achieving that goal—which may be quite unlike the goals their bosses in Accounting or Production had in mind when they seconded them to the team. Further, you will probably want to manage the new team's dynamics until its participants genuinely knit into a team, come to rely on each other, and start moving effectively toward their goal.

Assembling a team of this kind from among gifted people with initially competing loyalties and perspectives can make a remarkable difference in your change project. It is a great strategy—and a

CASE STUDY

SOUTHWEST AIRLINES: A COMPANY THAT THINKS NEW

Southwest Airlines demonstrates what can happen when a company unites a powerful shared vision with a culture of innovation. Southwest innovates as it "engineers" its business processes and practices. This approach is so integral to the way the company operates, so consistent with its philosophy and culture, that the term *reengineering* loses its context.

Southwest Airlines is soaring as many other airlines falter. It has maintained a steady stream of profits amid a disaster in general industry profitability. How has it accomplished this feat? It has done so by creating what we believe to be a truly world-class model in which employees *live* the principles underlying the company's success. Southwest manages to imbue these principles into its employees from the day they join, and the company is confident enough in its credo to present it in the lobby at headquarters—on a sign 15 feet high.

"Our people transformed an idea into a legend. That legend will continue to grow only so long as it is nourished by our people's indomitable spirit, boundless energy, immense goodwill, and burning desire to excel."

We know few companies whose employees understand better their company's strategy. In fact, most of Southwest's *customers*, given time, can rattle off something like: (*a*) short hauls, (*b*) frequent flights, (*c*) on-time arrivals, (*d*) no meals, (*e*) low fares. That is the strategy, and they stick to it. All key decisions are measured against it.

The culture at Southwest encourages new thinking. The casual dress code and atmosphere represent an invitation not to be lax but to think freely and creatively. People work hard but have fun, and this combination is understood by all to encourage innovation. Further supporting innovation, communications up, down, and across the company are wide open. Employees often write to Chairman Herb Kelleher to suggest changes. He and his group listen, and they respond. The environment fosters *new* thinking and cultivates *good* thinking.

Southwest's frequent flier program is a case in point—a brilliantly successful example of ignoring the conventions of the day. No challenging one. Cross-functional teams have advantages and disadvantages. The chief advantage, as we have said, is disparate points of view, yielding a series of overlaps that ultimately model your company as a whole. However, cross-functional teams do not readily have a common basis of fact and philosophy for reaching consensus. Like individuals, teams learn and adapt only through trial by experience. They need to learn to construct new frame-

"me-too" awards program here. The company has designed a program that meets the real needs and desires of its customers—of all customers, those using the program and those who do not. Recall how most major airlines' frequent flier programs work. You sign up by completing an application. When the company receives your application, clerks enter your membership into the system, and you soon begin receiving monthly notifications of miles accumulated, awards available, and so on.

However, operating in this way, the airlines maintain records for tens and even hundreds of thousands of *infrequent* fliers. They incur information-processing costs, mailing costs, and so on, without necessarily analyzing what all this activity buys them, what it costs, or how it impacts their pricing.

After researching what people really want in a frequent flier program and carefully weighing the best means of meeting—but not necessarily exceeding—customer needs, Southwest introduced its Company Club program. When you sign up, a Southwest agent hands you an application, just like any other airline. However, on this application there are 16 empty squares (if you're about to take a Southwest flight, the agent will stamp one of them). It is *your* task to carry this application with you on your next 15 flights. When you've taken your obligatory 16 flights, and 16 squares are stamped, *then* you become a member of the Company Club and immediately receive your first reward: a free ticket (not a complex menu of options).

The strategy is inspired and inspiring. It exemplifies big idea implementation. Resisting conventional wisdom, Southwest figured out how to give customers what they want—but not more. The company gracefully shifted the information-processing duties for all infrequent fliers (and those new to the airline) onto the customer's shoulders. And while you may think this contrary to the principles of customer service, it turns out to be well accepted. Customers just don't mind. And, like us, many people lose the application after five or six boxes are stamped and have to start all over! Southwest saves money and passes on some of the savings in the form of lower fares.

works and to populate their concepts with unshakable facts. When these facts do not fit the current paradigm, the team has to backpedal, reexamine, and innovate, rather than ignore the facts.

Real leadership on your part and commitment from both the individuals and the organization will be necessary. Participation in a team of this kind is a full-time job for the duration, and these folks will need to work as if their lives depend on it. It may suit

THE COURAGE OF HER CONVICTIONS

One of the largest corporate travel companies in the world assembled a team to rethink its entire core service delivery process. The team included people from marketing, project management, operations, and MIS, as well as staff from a sister division that did similar work in a different way. Through dialogue with the other team members, each participant became

acutely aware of the needs of other parts of the organization—needs that had never been acknowledged or, at best, had been given short shrift.

Over several months, these representatives of competing functions and divisions forged a common bond that enabled them to propose solutions that were necessary, although unpopular with some supervisors. One team member, a highly regarded director, had the misfortune of having her office near those of several senior colleagues who felt threatened by the project. These managers would stop her as she walked by, grill her about details of the ongoing project, urge her to tone down her recommendations for change.

The project director recognized this unwelcome and unwarranted influence—and the risk that it would lead to watered-down solutions. He asked the senior executive sponsor to remind the team that its thinking had to be new, and it didn't matter if the sensibilities of one or another interest group in the organization were offended, provided the team's recommendations truly enhanced the company's delivery of services.

This powerful message put to rest the director's fear of the demons down the hall. She was a key mover in developing innovative, principled, and successful recommendations by the team. And those recommendations called for substantial change. The organization was turned on its side, transforming the company from one tuned to the hierarchy of management to one driven by the voice of its customers. Functional structures were eliminated as multidisciplinary client service teams were put in place. Profits are climbing to new highs.

your purpose—we recommend this—to let team members know their performance on the team will be the basis of their evaluation and compensation while they are a part of the change effort. The success or failure of the change effort will be a factor in this. The team calls both for their full-time commitment and for much sensitivity to team dynamics. They will need to identify themselves as team members in team activities and as they move through the larger organization. They have a new identity—badges aren't required, but a clear sense of purpose and membership is.

While this exercise is not easy for anyone, sometimes a word from above can be the added motivation a team needs to stick together, as the case study on the facing page clearly shows.

GIVE THE TEAM A CHANCE

Put the group members to work at once. Involve them in the data-gathering and analytic phases of the effort so that they have a solid grounding in the facts upon which their recommendations must eventually be made. Dramatic change cannot be built upon analysis provided solely by staff analysts because it puts too great a distance between decisions and the fields subject to decision. Team members should talk directly with customers, crunch and interpret numbers—whatever needs to be done. In this way they will view the problems broadly, feel the human aspects through direct contact, and develop an insider's grasp of the numbers.

Then, as your team begins its work, move the entire team to a new location. Don't let team members remain at their old desks, near former bosses and responsibilities. For a time, move the entire group to a new location. Moving them will strengthen their bonds with one another and diminish old loyalties that now might get in the way. By this simple topographic strategy, you make unbiased recommendations much more likely to emerge.

> **Team members must be encouraged to think openly, not moderating their ideas in fear of later reprisals from their "local" supervisors. It is best when the CEO can make assurances to the team personally.**

And team members must be encouraged to think openly, not moderating their ideas in fear of later reprisals from their "local" supervisors. It is best when the CEO can make assurances to the team personally.

USE ALL THE LEVERS

Too often, promising new solutions are rejected out of hand and not seriously studied because the team imagines that the solutions are out of bounds. Similarly, the team may fail to look in directions that its members consider out of bounds. Both of these errors represent failures to focus on *all the levers of change* rather than the one or two that, due to their backgrounds, team members may regard as their province.

Any change project has a set of variables you might wish to change. Changes can be implemented through new processes, new technologies, new organizational structures, and so on: a limited set. Despite the basic simplicity of the options, few change teams consider all these levers to be "in play." Classically, they jump directly to technology solutions. Technology *is* a powerful enabler, but companies too often look to it to carry the entire burden of performance improvement. To create balanced solutions, your team needs to search for promising solutions related to all the levers of change. They might ask, for example: What if we were to tear up our organization chart and design a new one based on adding value to customer service first, last, and always? What if we were to find means of cost-effectively *tripling* the positive impact of our training programs? What if we segmented our customers differently? See Chapter One for more discussion on the levers of change.

> **Expose your team members to what is going on at other companies; see to it that they talk with the best thinkers within your company; encourage them to survey the available literature on best practices.**

ASK "WHAT IF?"

"What if" is at the center of any change project. What if a purchase didn't have to go through three approvals? . . . if a customer knew exactly what to do when a product doesn't work properly? . . . if a process wasn't under the jurisdiction of five different departments? Roger von Oech has a what-if we particularly like: "What if we had seven fingers on each hand?"[2] As he points out, this would be likely to change everything we do, from the kinds of music we write (would Beethoven's "Moonlight Sonata" have been the same if our hands had another half-octave stretch?) to the way we count (would we still use the decimal system if one finger didn't equal one-tenth?). Take the straitjacket off how things have been done until now. Ask what if.

BUILD BIG FROM SMALL

Every once in a while someone comes up with a really big, new idea. Fiber-optic cable, gene therapies for previously incurable diseases, the Hubble space telescope, the personal computer, and VisiCalc (the original spreadsheet) are recent examples. Such ideas,

[2] Ibid., p. 70.

when implemented, have enormous impact, and there is no reason to exclude the possibility that your change team will propose ideas of this magnitude. On the other hand, they also need to be aware of the power of small but important ideas or innovations linked together into a single big idea. If you explore this terrain with your team, you will almost certainly discover that each has been harboring one or more ideas of modest scope that, taken together, can have great impact. The innovative changes your company needs may not be a single "BIG idea"—it may be built, brick upon brick, from the smaller dreams of your change team.

BENCHMARK INTELLIGENTLY

An essential early insight in driving innovative change through your organization is the recognition that you are not alone in searching for big ideas. There are many great ideas out there, and they are available to you for the taking. This reality has fueled the current explosion in benchmarking. Smart managers know that it is too easy to become insular in their thinking. Benchmarking can be a very powerful means of initiating change because it exposes your managers to new ideas and to challenging performance standards achieved by other companies within and beyond your industry. One of the most positive results of benchmarking can be a fundamental culture shift in which your employees begin to understand the importance of continuous improvement and become more accepting of "best practices" employed by others. Expose your team

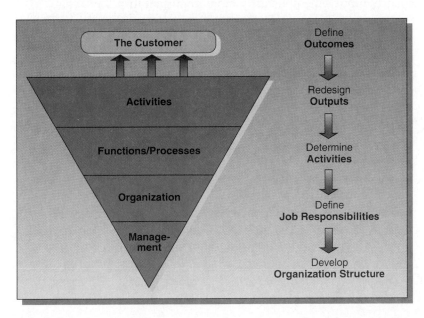

**FIGURE 8.2
THINK FROM THE
CUSTOMER BACK**

Challenge your people to do more than just build solutions on the shoulders of existing models. Ask yourselves what outcomes you want to achieve relative to your customer. Then, and only then, consider what outputs you need to create to achieve those outcomes. The rest follows from there.

members to what is going on at other companies; see to it that they talk with the best thinkers within your company; encourage them to survey the available literature on best practices, and so on. Make yourselves available to peers; you may have the big idea they need and the favor will more than likely be returned.

CREATE ANALOGIES

It is a struggle for most people to conceive of a future much different from today. To force new thinking and try on new concepts, *analogy* is one of the most powerful tools available. A good change team will create half-a-dozen commonsense analogies to describe new concepts, and the best of their analogies will be key to selling those concepts up and down the organizational ladder.

Reengineering is a good example of analogy at work. Much of process reengineering is nothing more than applying proven manufacturing concepts to business process environments. Concept building by analogy with existing models observed elsewhere in the organization or disclosed by benchmarking offers a shortcut for your own change processes. Analogy can spur new thinking, promote more and better risk-taking, and provide persuasive arguments for change.

TEST HYPOTHESES

In taking this course, however, remember that existing models are more than just anecdotes and a benchmark. The "how" of performance improvement is vastly more important than the "what." Expose the team to the full range of case facts and analysis. During this initial period of fact building, the team should be encouraged to develop and try new ideas. One fruitful strategy is to use the hypothesis/implication form of investigation, borrowed from the methods of science, in which the team formulates a hypothesis about the problem, then posits and tests a possible solution. As the fact base continues to build, this process of hypothesizing, and projecting and testing solutions, should be systematically pursued.

Hypotheses can be adjusted and retested against newly acquired facts. New analytic needs and data requirements will be identified if and when hypotheses prove wanting or projected solutions crash. The team is not circling repetitively; it is spiraling upward toward convincing hypotheses and solutions that demand to be taken out into the organization. During this stage of the team's work, you are more than likely to find it useful to involve external experts who can participate in the process of hypothesis/implication on the basis of their experience of benchmark achievements at other organizations. The analogies they bring will contribute to your own success in changing your organization— although it is always worth remembering the example of Southwest Airlines' successful frequent flier program, which runs counter to analogy, benchmark, and tradition. External experts may help you grasp what you *do not* wish to do, and this too can be a valuable contribution.

ESTABLISH STRETCH PERFORMANCE TARGETS

People are naturally more motivated when they have a goal. Unfortunately, not every goal presses toward the kind of break-through performance that most of us want from change projects. Demanding stretch goals will provide a powerful signal to every-one that, for this project, business as usual won't cut it. By target-ing what may seem an outrageous level of performance, you will force everyone to look at the issues in wholly new ways. They will have no alternative. They will know they can't possibly come up with viable solutions if they rely on past models. On the other hand, if you set comfortable goals, you will be tempting the team to adopt solutions that are already near at hand—and not especially effective.

> **By targeting what may seem an outrageous level of perfor-mance, you will force every-one to look at the issues in wholly new ways.**

Consider introducing new performance measures and goals beyond the familiar norms of your organization. Clarify the link between these new demands and the strategic and financial results required for the company's long-term success. You must be able to articu-late exactly how things will be better when the goals are met. Be specific: *The goal of becoming "more customer-focused" is vague; achieving 98 percent repeat purchases is not.*

INVOLVE YOUR PEOPLE

Employee involvement is one of the organization's best resources for performance improvement. Taking advantage of this resource requires management leadership, mutual respect, and training. Employees need to know they are key resources. Use employee focus groups liberally. They will uncover important facts, insights, and feelings that the team simply would not otherwise uncover. Focus group discussions are also very efficient. If they are infor-mal—lasting only an hour or so—you can conduct many. In this way a large number of people, representing a wide cross section of the employee base, can be polled. You will have much better data; they will know their views matter.

Use Organizational Tryouts

Once the team has agreed on the value of a big idea that has taken shape through its work, and once senior management has approved the fundamental idea, it should be communicated across and at many levels of the organization to develop feedback. Document clearly the core team's concept; solicit opinions; encourage tough questions that will help to improve the idea. Each group should feel free to challenge from its own perspective and to raise issues believed to have gone unaddressed. This is a tryout. Its purpose is to surface neglected issues needing to be considered now—before they have an opportunity to become obstacles to change. It also permits important constituencies to enhance the concept from additional points of view.

A by-product of this process is the opportunity to attain organizational buy-in as outsiders become insiders through their involvement in recommendations. Although this is a grass-roots exercise, not a presentation to senior decision makers who are presumably already insiders, the change team organizing this round of communication should be certain to include all those who are influential in shaping the organization's will to act—not necessarily all senior executives. The shop floor head and the chief of Accounts Receivable may influence hundreds of people. If you can win this group over, you're probably on the right course, and you have gained some powerful lobbyists.

The recommendation remains the responsibility of the team. Tryouts are not designed to water down a coherent recommendation, only to make it better. They may need to defend its substance, and they should do so vigorously when appropriate. After the tryout is concluded, the proposal should be revised to incorporate the key issues raised and additional ideas proposed. By the time the finished proposal is formally reviewed in front of appropriate senior committees or the board, large numbers of staff have been involved, many people have bought in, and most objections will have been raised and substantively addressed. If these preliminaries are properly done, final approval to move ahead should be anticlimactic.

Act New

The need to "act new" can get lost as the team becomes focused on implementing a radical new idea. Big ideas are rarely implemented from one day to the next. As a consequence of necessarily incremental change, for long periods most people will have one foot in the old world and the other in the new. This phenomenon can defeat a big idea, and you will need to manage against it.

The implementation plan needs to include not only a clear schedule to begin replacing the old way of doing things but also detailed guidance on how the organization can and must begin "acting new." It should identify substantial changes that can be put into practice while the systems or infrastructure for large-scale change remain under development. By rolling out change in phases throughout the company, with formal announced cut-over dates accompanied by new reporting structures or policies, the implementation team is pressured for results—and the larger organization is forced to recognize the imperative of starting to "act new."

PUTTING IT ALL TOGETHER

We have heard over and over again from individuals involved in change efforts that a given idea isn't new: "We've looked at that before and it didn't work." The corporate dumpster is filled with good ideas that were never given a chance. If you expect to achieve large-scale organizational change—if you expect to persuade people to take great risks, perhaps even to put their careers on the line—you must give them a clear and pressing reason, and you must give them a straightforward (not necessarily simple) way to change. The change team that has been the focus of this chapter offers the most effective means of identifying big, new ideas, of validating them through organizational tryout, of selling them to senior management, and of implementing them with a minimum of difficulty.

> **The recommendation remains the responsibility of the team. Tryouts are not designed to water down a coherent recommendation, only to make it better. They may need to defend its substance, and they should do so vigorously when appropriate.**

Through clarity, shared commitment to change, and the inherent wisdom of changes contemplated and the process for achieving them, the odds for success can be dramatically improved. Take time to lay the groundwork for your innovation effort. Take time to see it through. The result will be well worth the wait.

The hero of this chapter is the change team. The intelligence, method, and personal courage of its participants—at least of those who prove themselves and serve for the duration—set them apart as heirs apparent for senior management responsibilities. The change team is a school for higher management. And when some

of its members ultimately hold the reins of power, they too will
have to remember the importance of thinking big, acting new.
They in turn will have to consider empowering a change team, if
the business demands it, to transform not only the way other people
do their jobs but also the way they themselves do their jobs.

CHECKLIST   THINKING BIG, ACTING NEW

___ Begin by believing large-scale, wide-scope change is both possible and imperative.

___ Prove the imperative for change by setting stretch performance targets and articulating how things will be better when the goals are met.

___ Cultivate the innovation mind-set in your people: ask for it, respond to it, reward it. Promote the people who have it and use it. Never punish someone for trying to have and use a good idea, even if the idea doesn't ultimately win its way.

___ Look far and wide for innovation. Bring together, explore, and then integrate diverse and unconventional points of view. If you ask the same old people, you'll get the same old answers.

___ To help teams of diverse people with disparate backgrounds work together, give them the same goal, and make them all accountable for achieving it.

___ Immerse the team in their current environment while they analyze its problems. But when it comes time to design solutions, take them away—literally—from the distractions and pressures of their current jobs and bosses. You'll be amazed at how they loosen their own and each others' biases and constraints.

___ Remember to explore all the levers of change.

___ Ask "what if . . . ?" Use some "what if?" exercises to loosen up the team and get it into "what if?" mode.

___ Combine small ideas and previous innovations to find one big idea.

___ Borrow intelligently, as possible and as appropriate. Benchmark to find best practices. Remember, benchmarking can also tell you what doesn't work.

___ Test solutions. Use focus groups. Both provide real-world feedback before you brave the new world.

___ Give people some guidance for the dark netherworld of transition time, between the time when acting old was OK and when acting new becomes mandatory. Your best people—the ones who can't abide subpar performance—are the ones at most risk during this time.

NINE

Measuring Performance

usiness leaders today are almost constantly testing and reworking their company's strategies. However, they do not question and rework their company's performance measures with quite the same zest. Performance measures monitor the company's progress, tell employees what really matters, and underpin a realistic reward structure. When strategy and management techniques ranging from JIT to team organization run ahead of performance measures, odd things happen—bad things. This chapter recommends instituting a balanced set of measures focusing not only on results but also on processes. It argues for the value of keeping performance measures closely aligned with current strategies and objectives. And it provides a good deal of how-to in a discipline fundamental to successful change.

• • •

Imagine a stagecoach like the ones in movies about the Old West. Six frantic horses strain at the reins as the coachmaster cracks his whip, urging them on. Now imagine the horses all pulling *in different directions*! Chaos. The coach is sure to overturn; it may break up.

This high drama is not wholly unlike the sequence of events in most organizations when project resources (good people with good ideas and enthusiasm) are set in motion without clear and consistent performance measures. In our experience, no single factor so thoroughly undermines efforts to change an organization as do soft and fuzzy—or worse, conflicting—objectives and corresponding measures.

Accordingly, there is no more important chapter in this book. You can get everything else right, but if you deploy a poor set of measures (or none at all), any positive change accomplished will soon be undermined by the inefficiencies of your organization as managers chase an inconsistent or conflicting set of targets. Getting performance measures right will confirm and grow your success. Getting them wrong has to be out of the question.

Restructure, recapitalize, reorganize—that's where the action was in the 80s, and with each new action came new needs to measure performance. The problem was that no one seemed to be looking at the old measures to determine whether they were still relevant. The result: New measures were put in place alongside the old, and most companies ended up with far too many, certainly far too many to support their current businesses.

Consider the issues facing this soft drink bottler. Upon securing a new sale (the installation of a vending machine or soda fountain for a new customer), the sales organization would obtain the signed sales contract and then pass the order on to a maintenance/installation group responsible for installing the equipment. Installation was often completed successfully two or more weeks *after* the promised date, usually after several on-premise visits. Because of such frequent breaches in customer agreements, sales were being lost to competitors capable of getting sites up and operational more responsively.

Performance measures are a primary strategy deployment tool.

The company's measures and business practices virtually reinforced poor performance. The salesperson was commissioned upon obtaining the signed sales contract, and thus had little incentive to help coordinate the installation. The installers were measured on the number of calls they were able to make in an eight-hour day. Both groups were performing well, based on the measures. But the measures were no good. Customers were not being served and the company was losing business—while the measures remained happy with what was occurring. Measures should become very sad when business is dropping off.

The changes required in the measurement system were simple yet effective. First, both operating units were given a "shared measure." The salespeople are now paid *after* the successful installation of vending or fountain equipment. The installers are measured on the number of successful installations occurring on schedule and in the first on-premise visit. With this shared measure, both units are motivated to do what is required to satisfy customers at the least cost (the cost-effectiveness arises from the economy of a single on-premise installation visit rather than multiple visits).

In creating a balanced set of internally *and* externally focused measures for your business, we suggest you begin by taking an inventory of your company's portfolio of performance measures. Then map them to your corporate strategies, and take a tough attitude in judging whether each measure is truly supportive of the company's vision and mission. Often, a significant percentage of an organization's measures conflict with or fail to support existing strategies. At a company where we analyzed selected reports sent to senior executives, we were able to identify *600 different measures*. Given more time, we believe we could have uncovered still others! You have to wonder how the company's managers and employees knew what was important. Overpopulation is counter-strategy, no matter what the company's vision and strategy may be.

Performance measures are a primary strategy deployment tool. As such, they must be linked to strategy to ensure that the right signals are being sent by senior management. When those signals are received loud and clear, employees know what matters most. Many strategies are conceptual in character and too broad in scope to provide guidance on a day-to-day basis, but performance measures are narrowly focused and pragmatic. They matter. They are used to evaluate individual performance and they are often used to determine compensation. Now that's real!

Performance measures are also a strong force in shaping the culture of an organization. The underlying values of an organization are often influenced by, and a direct reflection of, key performance measures.

In driving change in your organization, performance measures are your best friends. There is no more powerful means of communicating to stakeholders that things are going to be different from this point forward than to reshape what is being measured.

WHAT GETS MEASURED GETS DONE?

Not always—not when performance measures conflict with one another or when there are too many. Most organizations today have far too many measures, typically because measures are still in place that were developed to support strategies and initiatives long since discarded. Inefficiency results because the ghost of management past remains the measure of management present.

For example, team measures are consistent with today's drive to attain world-class performance. Yet we have found that even after establishing teamwork programs, many companies still have measures that are souvenirs of older strategies that rewarded individual effort.

MEASURES ARE INTEGRAL TO CHANGE

Companies that want to move ahead in the 90s by undertaking broad-based change must include review of their measurement system in their quest for improved performance. A balanced set of measures facilitates changes occurring in an organization because it covers all aspects of the business—people development, product development, manufacturing, marketing, and stakeholder satisfaction.

Yet wholesale revision of performance measures is not an action that most organizations willingly undertake. They tend to do so incrementally, as top management becomes dissatisfied with the pace of improvement and as operational managers rebel against measures that no longer make sense. Granted, stepwise transformation is not very glamorous, but in one way or another the introduction of meaningful measures must occur. If you do not adjust your measures, you may make change nearly impossible to achieve. Consider, for example, the situation of a manufacturing company that wants to reduce inventory through migrating to just-in-time (JIT) production scheduling. If the plant implementing this strategy continues to be measured on overhead absorption, the measures will probably report that the plant should be building inventory during slack periods. Clearly, this measure is out of step with a modern manufacturing system such as JIT and should be reexamined.

> **A goal-focused measurement system is the best vehicle for institutionalizing targeted changes in the management process and galvanizing management action.**

INSTITUTIONALIZING CHANGE

Change projects can lead to isolated improvement at best if proper performance measurements are not concurrently implemented. Without a set of relevant goal-focused measures, you will find it nearly impossible to tell whether your organization is operating in step with its overall strategies. However, the most important reason for paying close attention to performance measures is that a goal-focused measurement system is the best vehicle for institutionalizing targeted changes in the management process and galvanizing management action. It can make your people surer and braver, your organization stronger and more successful. In short, it is the key to transforming your organization. Management tools do not get much better than this.

CREATING A BALANCED SET OF MEASURES

No measure is fully adequate apart from others; only a balanced set tells the whole story of what is going on in the organization. A balanced set includes a cross section of performance measurements: financial, nonfinancial; cost, noncost; internal, external; process,

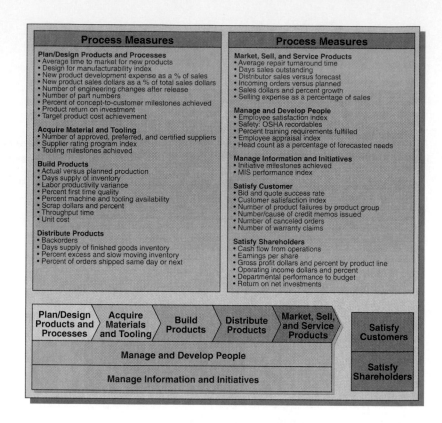

results. Senior executives and managers guiding the business against a balanced set of measures will find themselves with their hands on all the controls required to implement strategy and achieve objectives.

Balance can only be defined in relation to a company's specific strategies and value chain (i.e., key processes). Therefore, even direct competitors in the same industry are unlikely to have identical sets of measurements. Figure 9.1 illustrates a balanced set developed by one of our clients. It encompasses all elements of this manufacturing company's value chain and supports the current strategy. Careful review of these measures is well worth your time. They convey this client's vision of achieving high levels of customer satisfaction through cost reduction, high quality, and speed, and they correspond to each element of the company's value chain. They are a mix of statistical and financial measurements.

> **The rethinking of the organization's performance measures should be entrusted to a cross-functional team of high-level managers representing the far corners of the organization.**

And they reinforce the company's new product development strategy. In other words, they are a balanced set. Further, they are measurements, not data categories, because each has a goal and is subject to regular reporting. Figure 9.2 gives another picture of a balanced set of measures that you may find helpful.

CHOOSING MEASURES

The rethinking of the organization's performance measures should be entrusted to a cross-functional team of high-level managers representing the far corners of the organization. It is important to include those who can provide know-how in such areas as engineering, marketing, manufacturing, human resources, and information systems. The team should examine each proposed measure and develop a very brief definition of its purpose, and while doing so look for:

• **Relevance.** Does it have a significant, demonstrable relation to strategy and objectives?

• **Reliability.** Will the measure help identify the strengths and weaknesses of one or more business processes?

• **Clarity of naming system.** Is its purpose readily understandable by its name alone?

• **Availability of data.** Are the data necessary for computing this measure available at reasonable cost?

Once a measure has been selected, further work must be done to make sure that it is well defined and supported by an exact method for its calculation. For example, does a measure for product lead

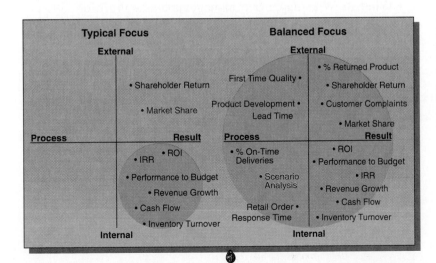

FIGURE 9.2
EMPLOYING A BALANCED SET OF PERFORMANCE MEASURES
The use of performance measures must be creative. Make certain that the measures are a balanced set focused on internal and external results *and* processes.

time define exactly when a development project begins and ends? To avoid scrappy confrontations—as opposed to productive debate—a Delphi approach can be used in the selection process.

HOW MANY MEASURES?

As we have suggested, the chances are good that your organization has outmoded, potentially harmful performance measures in place. Assuming that these are winnowed out, an organization will typically have from 40 to 60 performance measures based on its business activities and strategies, and mapped to each element of its value chain.

PRINCIPLES FOR SELECTING PERFORMANCE MEASURES

As your change teams think about the need for new measures, they should consider the following five basic principles:

PRINCIPLE 1. REEVALUATE EXISTING MEASURES

Even when measures are widely regarded as useless, they often stay in place for reasons related to management comfort. The known is often preferred to the unknown—even if it doesn't work. Your change team will need to guard against the influence of any or all of the following:

• **Fear.** What if the new set of measures doesn't work? We need something to fall back on until the new set is proven.

• **Ownership.** There is someone's name on that outdated measurement. He's important, let's not risk offending him.

• **What-if.** What happens if management asks for information based on the old system? This is the equivalent of reporting data based on the premise that the Earth is flat even after the reality of the Earth's curvature is known. The old, irrelevant statistics are still

FIGURE 9.3
SAMPLE PROCESS
MEASURES

Process Measures	Operational Strategies They Measure
• Number of products or services • Number of parts produced • Length of order fulfillment cycle • Length of order manufacturing cycle • Number of distribution points • Product development lead time • Number of engineering changes • Items passing quality standards • Unit cost • Number of suppliers • Supplier performance index • Number of invoices • Training hours achieved • Counseling frequency	• Differentiate the product from the competition • Serve the customer as a first priority • Develop technologically advanced products in an effective manner • Increase product line profitability • Procure material effectively • Establish a low-cost administrative structure • Develop human resources assets

CHAPTER NINE

calculated along with the new and relevant—just in case someone asks for them.

- **Rewards.** There were rewards tied to the old system; if they remain, then doing it the old way still makes sense.

- **Estimates.** Basing business decisions on estimates somehow seems less scientific than using "hard numbers"—even when underlying assumptions have been well documented and are understood.

PRINCIPLE 2. MEASURE IMPORTANT BUSINESS PROCESSES, NOT JUST RESULTS

Most results-oriented measures (which tend to be financially and internally focused and historical in nature) will indicate when there is a problem but probably will not help you diagnose it. You have to measure underlying business processes to see the whole picture and to gather stronger clues about potential fixes, should things go awry.

Most companies will benefit enormously from measuring variables in processes such as product development, manufacturing, marketing, employee development, and the like. If you improve the company's core business processes, then measures of customer and shareholder satisfaction (e.g., market share and ROI) will improve as well. Figure 9.3 shows a variety of process measures and indicates how they relate to operating strategies.

Revised measurement systems serve two purposes: to provide information about the effectiveness of business processes and to measure the ultimate results of these processes. Designing a new measurement system is complex, but using it correctly is even more difficult. We recall, for example, the experience of a company that shifted from concentrating on results to measuring processes more vigorously.

> **Even when measures are widely regarded as useless, they often stay in place for reasons related to management comfort.**

PRINCIPLE 3. MEASURES SHOULD FOSTER GOAL-DRIVEN TEAMWORK

Shared process measurements create an environment of goal-driven teamwork—and this is good. Modern corporations are too complex for one individual or department to shoulder it all. To get things done, teams of people must grab the oars and row in unison.

Consider backlog, for example. As a measure, backlog indicates items not shipped when the customer asked for them. As backlog rises, it tells us customers are becoming increasingly

BALANCED MEASURES

The company's problems were obvious. One-fifth of its market share was gone; the company had reorganized almost every year; the balance sheet was in a state of disrepair, and line managers were demoralized by constant attrition.

Recognizing that it could not live with the status quo, management undertook a series of actions to turn things around. The first step was to achieve a general awakening at the top of the house: Senior executives were brought to acknowledge the critical condition of the business. Absent real candor in this regard, many problems had simply not been addressed. Issues had been discussed, but the company's long tradition of success made it exceedingly difficult to hear the market's stiff messages. Measurements were unsound—no better than snippets of information that could be acted upon or ignored according to executive whim.

The atmosphere of awakening and truth telling began to spread through the organization. Slogans were abandoned in favor of honest assessment. And without misleading people, internal communications also looked to the future. Employees were urged to perceive the problems as opportunities—the toughest issues providing the greatest opportunities for long-term improvement. Suppressing information about problems was forcefully defined as counterproductive. In other words, the warning signals flashed by the company's measures could no longer be safely ignored.

A balanced set of measures had to be adopted by managers, who understood that a single measure could easily generate wrong conclusions. For example, avoiding an engineering change to escape the scrutiny of measurement could result in excess manufacturing cost or, worse, dissatisfied customers. Historically, if a measurement had indicated a problem, management would either ignore it or call on the carpet the manager whose numbers had turned unfavorable. But as measurements began to be used in a balanced manner, executives understood that the root cause of a problem might lie elsewhere. For example, quality might be inadequate because the designers ignored a needed engineering change. The company began to use root-cause

dissatisfied with service levels. Backlog is an obviously useful measurement—more useful than many companies realize in the sense that, properly read, it also tells us something about the effectiveness of processes along the entire supply chain and about analysis across boundaries on a routine basis to pinpoint process shortcomings wherever they showed up.

More fundamental still, the notion of data had to be separated from the notion of measurement. Regulatory requirements generated certain data, but these data could no longer be presumed, rather carelessly, to be performance measures reflecting management's strategy and objectives. *Data were simply data.*

Effective performance measures were understood to be related to external benchmarks, directed toward specific goals, and designed to serve management information needs. And, most important, key players now agreed that measurements have a *goal*, while data are just data until absorbed into an analytic framework characterized by goals. While in the new environment a manager could access as much data as needed, measurements came to be associated with goals—and the manager was expected to achieve them. In this way the company learned to separate data and measurements. The difference: Was a goal present or not?

It took six months to move beyond discussing historical financial data and develop real measurement information that could help managers address short-term problems. Meetings focused on the root causes of problems and the future implications of those problems. As measurement information was brought more in line with key data items in the business plan, the measures showed the plan itself had flaws, and important changes in planning were initiated.

Not only did operational matters become more important in these meetings, but also strengthened concern for product development and customer satisfaction focused attention on the outside world. Managers discovered that they could report problems without retribution. The questions at key meetings became: Is the problem important? Has the root cause of the problem been identified? How will your actions to resolve the problem affect other measurements? Will solving the problem enhance the business plan? What help do you need? In the past, problems had been shunted from group to group because no one wanted them. Now, units actually sought recognition for their problem-solving skills—and this meant they had to solve problems and demonstrate the solutions for all to appreciate.

the levels of interdepartmental coordination and teamwork. To have the right product on hand when the customer wants it takes effort from the sales force to forecast demand, from purchasing managers who buy raw material, from manufacturing teams that make the product, and from customer service professionals watching inventory levels. Indirectly, backlog measures the level of teamwork among all these groups. If backlog is getting out of hand, management should know where to begin asking questions.

There are other meaningful measures of teamwork—for example, new product development lead time. Marketing, Engineering, Logistics, Manufacturing, and Sales all have to pull together to meet the product's target release date. First-time quality not only measures quality, as advertised, but may also reflect the efficacy of such activities as training, machine maintenance, purchasing, process engineering, and supervision.

In a recent assignment, we helped a client bring its measures in line with a new operating model. An important aspect of the client's strategy was greater emphasis on teamwork. Yet all the existing measures focused on individual accomplishment. A flurry of remedial communications to the organization stressed team selling, but executives were still measured largely on revenue contribution, and this in turn reinforced old behaviors. The changes in behavior sought by the client called for increased collaboration; the measures, however, encouraged individuals to maintain their independence from others. The problem was central and curable.

Another client company, which maintains its cost position by taking full advantage of economies of scale, relies on geographically diverse units to work together to complete the company's extended value chain. Since interunit linkages are so critical in this configuration, senior management developed a teamwork index to assess formally how well the various units worked together to achieve the overall business plan. One manufacturing plant even measured its relationships with major suppliers as well as with the company's marketing and product design groups. These measures highlighted areas for improvement. This awareness, in turn, reinforced all participants' focus on the importance of teamwork. (For instance, Manufacturing may think that all is well in its working relationship with Marketing, but Marketing's report card on Manufacturing may highlight a lack of communication that reduces *overall company* effectiveness.)

PRINCIPLE 4. MEASURES SHOULD BE AN INTEGRATED SET, BALANCED IN THEIR APPLICATION

To be effective, a measurement system must be designed as an integrated set derived from company strategy. Most organizations try to minimize cost, improve quality, reduce lead times, and provide adequate return on investment. They develop specific corporate projects to support these strategies—and these strategies, in turn, should be the basis for their measurement set. Where skill and judgment enter in is the selection of a few important measures capable of focusing the organization on today's strategies, not yesterday's. No single measurement is perfect—hence our frequent return to the phrase "set of measures." The set of measures should be carefully selected and monitored to ensure that it is moving the organization toward implementing its critical strategies.

PRINCIPLE 5.   MEASURES SHOULD HAVE AN EXTERNAL FOCUS WHENEVER POSSIBLE

A common internal yardstick in most organizations is year-to-year performance comparison. Such comparison can be taken to a micro level: division, department, group, even individual. Let no one argue against this approach. On the other hand, it does not paint the whole picture—it does not tell you whether your organization is reducing costs more slowly than your competitors, or improving the quality of a product or service that has been at least temporarily leapfrogged by a competitor, or gaining market share in an area that others are abandoning. These are all external concerns, and they mean much.

Below you will find the outline of a report used by one of our clients. It combines an intelligent internal perspective with *a view of the outside world.*

Internal:
    Revenue
    Operating income
    Cash flow
    Asset utilization

> **No single measurement is perfect—hence our frequent return to the phrase "set of measures."**

External:
    Detailed part cost comparison versus competitors
    Capital redeployment techniques used by others
    Items in business press about competitors
    Measurements of customer complaints
    Thought pieces concerning innovative approaches to product distribution
    Prices achieved for bellwether items

The information in this report shows that the executives are clearly aware of the danger of forgetting about the real world beyond their organization's four walls.

GOOD PERFORMANCE MEASURES BUILD ENTHUSIASM

The meeting started like any other. Materials were handed out; people tried to set aside their earlier concerns of the day to focus on the topic at hand. The introductions began—few suspecting that this would be a key event for the reengineering work sponsored by the controller's group. The purpose of the meeting was to brainstorm and identify a comprehensive set of measures to gauge the group's performance.

Several objective-setting sessions and many customer interviews had preceded this meeting. The discussion began with a review of what had been agreed upon earlier as the group's objectives. They had been drawn along four dimensions: cost, quality, speed, and information access. As an administrative group with internal customers only, the employees present at this meeting were unaccustomed to thinking of the services they provided in these dimensions. Performance in the past had been largely a function of having answers when they were asked questions and controlling departmental costs.

During the prior two years, the company had been pursuing a corporatewide TQM program. Executive training classes had already gone a long way toward educating the company's executives and managers about the importance of recasting the measures they used. They knew measures must be attuned to internal and external customer requirements, must be more process-oriented, and must be much more challenging.

As the meeting continued, one could sense momentum building as the group genuinely

---

Well-selected measures can help to drive real change. The case study on these pages provides insight into just how powerfully measures can motivate staff members to reach for greater performance.

MEASURES TIED TO REWARDS

As you significantly modify performance measures, a new reward system becomes necessary—tied, naturally, to the new performance measures. The types of measures we have recommended in this chapter are directed toward making the profit pie bigger, not toward slicing the pie differently or whipping more air into the heavy cream.

Our car recently broke down. The magnificent machine just wouldn't budge. Its engine turned over hoarsely. A mechanic came by, lifted the hood, poked around. Nothing, nothing. Then, with the

pursued the development of a challenging set of measures. They were almost visibly making an emotional and intellectual break with the past. When the meeting eventually concluded and aggressive stretch targets were in place, all participants understood there could be no backing down. The controller's group had driven some very key stakes into the ground. They had agreed on objectives, measures, and stretch targets. The measures were linked directly to their objectives; the measures were quantifiable; and, most important, they reached out directly to their customers by measuring what matters most to that key constituency.

The agreements reached at that meeting created powerful performance incentives through a set of intelligent measures closely linked to goals. The logic and integrity of these measures ignited an enthusiasm that, in turn, heightened the group members' interest in challenging themselves. None of this would have occurred had the measures retained their traditionally internal focus on budget measures. Turned on, the group actually developed much more challenging and aggressive goals than had been expected of them.

This client is now at work revamping practices, revising processes, and developing technology solutions aimed squarely at meeting the objectives they themselves set. They are implementing real change—and, beyond that, they are institutionalizing continuous improvement.

instinct of a real professional, he wobbled a miniature fuse in its slightly less miniature sleeve. Took it out, wiped its contacts on his shirt, put it back. Vroom! Problem solved. One small part—fingernail size—had stopped a multi-ton car. Performance measures are of this kind. They are embedded in the inner workings of the organization. You count on them to do what they're supposed to do. They are a small part of the organization's functioning—but if they aren't what they need to be, the magnificent machine may not budge.

CHECKLIST   MEASURING PERFORMANCE

___ Inventory your measures. Match them to your strategies. Discard those that are no longer relevant or that are duplicative. Notify managers and employees when those measures are no longer in use. Stop the system or process that does the measuring.

___ Consider changing to a new measurement system at the beginning of a business cycle or evaluation period, so that people complete a cycle or evaluation period with the performance evaluation and compensation system they expect.

___ Develop process performance measures, not just results measures. Results measures tell you *how you did*. Process measures tell you *how you are doing*, in time to change if necessary to get the results you want. The right process measures serve as predictors of results and can be used to manage the business in real time.

___ Use process performance measures and goals to motivate teams to work together.

___ Balance measures so you have an appropriate mix of financial and nonfinancial, cost and noncost, internal and external, process and results measures.

___ Compare performance in all measure areas against external benchmarks.

___ Measure performance in all key cross-functional business processes: not just operational and financial processes, but product and people development as well. Define processes carefully so that accountability for performance is clear.

___ Use performance measures to link what people do well on a day-to-day basis to the company's overall objectives.

___ To help measures pass easily into use,

    ___ Be sure that performance information or data are easily accessible for measurement.

    ___ Change reward, incentive, and compensation systems to reflect the new measures (remove incentives associated with discarded measures).

    ___ Pilot use of the new performance measurement system for part or all of a business cycle.

    ___ Assure people that you will not be asking for information from the old performance measurement system.

    ___ Don't underestimate the importance of a simple, easy-to-remember name that helps people recall what the measure is about.

Afterword

Not long ago a client asked one of our authors, the seasoned change services consultant, Ed Goll, just what he means by "managing change." Ed took a moment's thought, summarily reviewed his many client assignments over the past 15 years, and replied that it really means helping clients *manage courage*.

Much of change management distills to managing courage: summoning courage in yourself, in those around you, and in your organization's senior executives. As we observed some 180 pages ago, we have discovered that a deficit of courage is a major impediment to change. Without courage—on your part and that of many others—you cannot expect to effect the kind or level of positive change required by today's vastly more competitive business environment.

But *can you* manage courage? The short and necessary answer is "yes." A client half-seriously, half-jokingly shared an insight with us: "Some real part of the courage exhibited in defense of the Alamo had to do with the dearth of back doors." An extreme analogy—extremely truthful.

Think about the change effort in which you are a participant or leader right now. How many back doors have you noticed? Can managers opt out (overtly or covertly) by criticizing or hiding behind a muddled strategy? Can they claim to be newly empowered, and thus unilaterally perpetuate "as-is" behavior? Are they unconvinced that *they* must change along with others? Can they choose to respond to obsolete, but extant, performance measures?

We hope that the preceding chapters have equipped you with insight concerning the "back doors" and barriers that can impede change in your organization. We hope that the wisdom and techniques and, above all, the guiding principles underlying this book will summon additional courage in you. You will need it. But achieving your organizational objectives, and the personal satisfaction of doing so, will be well worth the effort.

AND ON THE SEVENTH DAY

The change process as we have proposed it is demanding. There is much at risk, many aspects that require unwavering attention, persevering care. There are many different stakeholder groups to acknowledge and move along the path of change. Pursued in this relentless, serious way, change management is hard work. It even changes the agents of change: You will surely gain a deeper understanding of your organization and of yourself.

We suggested at one point that change projects have a beginning, middle, and end. Like you, we know the slogans—success is a journey not a destination, and so on. The fact remains that sustaining positive change will require you to bundle your change initiatives into recognizable programs, even if those programs are carried out over a long period of time, and even if—as is often true—your long-lasting programs will need to be reinvented periodically to fit changing conditions, new strategies, and the like. The moment will nonetheless come when your objectives have been met.

This is the moment when you should take care of yourself and your team, and by this we mean something specific: Step back from what you and your colleagues have achieved, as if you were fine cabinetmakers taking in the beauty and soundness of the finished object. There is surely more work to do. But the "object"—the reengineered process, the pattern of empowerment, the job-changing technology migration—is a reality now evident in new levels of performance. In your heart of hearts, you know that given a second chance you would have done certain things differently. The reality differs a bit from the vision, but those differences, small enough, serve to remind you that to err is human and that your feet of clay are still size 6 or size 10, just as they were before all this began.

Still, the finished work is satisfying. You know that you and your team have made a difference, and you take pride in this. The new process works well. People are happy with it. Empowerment has already improved the bottom line and people now feel, rightly, that they own their jobs as partners in building the company's success. The sometimes maddening technology shift has given the company five or six years of room for growth, and the management information generated by the new system is already promoting that growth. Whatever your project, you see its results before you.

You have reached the seventh day. Monday will come soon enough—a new day full of new challenges. But this is still the seventh day. By taking time to appreciate and celebrate what has been accomplished, we send ourselves the most important message of all: such things *can* be done, and done well. Positive, lasting change—Better Change—can be accomplished. We are confident of this. You can be confident of it, too.

Summon your courage now. On the seventh day you'll be glad.

Index

Please send me information on Price Waterhouse's

_____ Presentation on keys to successful transformation

_____ Proprietary automated process analysis tool

_____ Online databases of information on best practices

_____ Facilitator's guide and materials for a Change Readiness Workshop

_____ Methodology and services for Change Integration®

_____ I would like more information/a phone call regarding _____
_____
_____

Name _____ Phone _____

Company _____

Address _____

City _____ State _____ Zip _____

Use bookmarks below to note special topics/ideas for future reference.

| 1 | 2 | 3 | 4 | 5 | 6 | 7 |

Price Waterhouse

Change Integration®
15301 Dallas Parkway
Suite 300
Dallas, Texas 75248

Use bookmarks
below to note
special topics/
ideas for future
reference.

7

6

5

4

3

2

1